The sixties were a time of peace
The seventies are bags stained with
grease

what about the bloody 80s.

To Pat
from Ron

Second Attempt

The sixties were a time of peacy
The eighties mere bags stained with grease
what happened to the bloody seventies!

Poems of the Sixties

edited by F E S FINN

with an introduction by NORMAN NICHOLSON

John Murray · Albemarle Street · London

INTRODUCTION

Had I been asked, ten or twenty years ago, to write an introduction to an anthology similar to this—*Poems of the Fifties* or *Poems of the Forties*—I would probably have begun by saying that most people looked on poetry as something far removed from ordinary life and thought of modern poetry, in particular, as being dry, harsh, almost unintelligible, with neither rhyme nor reason. Today there are signs of a change, and, at least among the young, poetry has suddenly come into fashion. This doesn't mean that more people are actually reading it, but, certainly, thousands more are now writing it! All over the country schools are producing poetry magazines or collections, while 'little magazines', often merely typed and duplicated, are printing new poems by the hundred. In many towns poets meet regularly in bookshops and pubs, and no protest meeting or pop festival, no sit-in or love-in is complete without someone jumping up to spout out his own verses.

And not only are people writing poetry, they are listening to it, too. This is specially true of the generation that listens to pop. In Liverpool and Newcastle, for instance, the local poets have a following almost as enthusiastic as that of the local pop-groups, and their lively, irreverent, impromptu style of verse, packed with parish-pump allusions and topical laughs, has drawn large audiences on regional television.

Nor is it just the pop poets who are getting a response. Many a middle-aged poet like me is now finding that people will listen to his poetry when they will not read it for themselves. And at the great international poetry readings, in places like the Albert Hall, thousands of people will cheer visiting poets even when they read in a language which scarcely anyone in the audience can understand.

I think the reason for all this is that, in an age of radio, cinema, the record player and television, poetry still remains the most personal of the arts. The novel is being replaced, for many people, by the television play, and music-making at home, by the record and the transistor. But the poem is still, primarily, a direct communication from man to man: not just the words on the page but the words spoken by the poet.

That, of course, is how poetry began, for it was essentially an oral art and was practised in many civilizations long before the people had learned the art of writing. Poetry is easier to learn by heart than prose. So it was used as a way of memorizing information and passing it down, by word of mouth, from generation to generation—things like the laws and customs of the tribe, proverbs and saws, or useful hints about housework:

A stitch in time
Saves nine,

or the weather:

A red sky at night—
The shepherd's delight.

Again, poetry, because of its rhythm and repetitions, often has an incantatory effect on the hearer, raising him to a state of great excitement. So it was used for all kinds of rituals and ceremonies, from the simplest children's games:

Eena, meena, mina, mo,
Catch a nigger by the toe;

to the most exalted religious liturgy:

O all ye works of the Lord, bless ye the Lord;
    praise him, and magnify him for ever.
O ye angels of the Lord, bless ye the Lord;
    praise him, and magnify him for ever.

As civilizations developed, verse forms became more complex, and poetry more sophisticated, with subtleties of meaning that could not be fully understood at one hearing alone. Poetry of that kind just had to be written down if it was to be preserved and enjoyed. But poets did not entirely forget the old oral tradition. Shakespeare wrote for an audience listening in a theatre; the blind Milton composed his poems in his head and dictated them to his secretary. At the same time there remained, until about a hundred years ago, a great mass of

vi

people who could not read at all. So far as they were concerned, novels, newspapers and the like just did not exist. *Their* stories were the ballads of Robin Hood, or folk songs and nursery rhymes, or the topical songs about murders, ghosts and mysteries sung in the streets of London. In those days, as in the early days of civilization, poetry was the literature of the illiterate.

With the coming of education for all, this oral tradition has almost died out. But now we seem to be trying to get back to it, to get back to a sense of poetry as the art of the spoken word, of the direct man-to-man communication between poet and hearer.

All of which is excellent in its way, but 'poetry' is a wide term and I have been using it very loosely. In fact, much of the verse of the new pop poets can't really be called poetry at all. Some of them, such as Brian Patten and Barry Mac-Sweeney, do show flashes of a genuine poetic sensibility, but most of them seem ready to throw away their considerable talents for the sake of the quick laugh, the stock response and instant applause. It is very easy for a young poet to rouse enthusiasm from a young audience by throwing in anti-Vietnam slogans, protests about war and the establishment, cheap laughs at religion, and plenty of ripe references to sex, television ads. and all the supermarket brands. Directness, spontaneity, informality, the lively image, the quick, arresting phrase, wit and humour, can all help to make a poem enjoyable and effective—but they don't make a poem in themselves. The trouble with much pop poetry is that it is *too* spontaneous! It is only the raw material of poetry; it has not been through the full imaginative process. Not long ago a teacher came to me with a batch of verses written by a very young pupil.

'They're no trouble to her,' he said. 'She just writes them straight off. They don't take her more than five minutes.'

'That's what they look like,' I said.

Now some of the poems in this collection may look as if

they, too, hadn't taken more than five minutes, but don't be misled by this. For *apparent* spontaneity is the result of very skilful art, and most of the poems in this volume (except a handful about which the editor and I can cheerfully disagree) have been through the imaginative process all right. Directness, informality, the lively image, the quick, arresting phrase, wit and humour—in fact, all those things which people enjoy in the pop poets—are found here in poems which really *are* poems, poems which have the hall-mark of the craftsmen stamped on them.

There are poems of protest, poems of rebellion, poems which cast a critical or sardonic or sympathetic look over the world as it is today. And these latter are by no means all written by young men. For, though this anthology is called *Poems of the Sixties*, it is not confined to poets of one generation. It is, in fact, a collection of poets, all of whom were writing in the Sixties, whose ages vary from just over twenty to just under eighty. William Plomer, for instance, might have been labelled as a poet of the Thirties, since his poems first began to appear beside those of W. H. Auden, Stephen Spender and Cecil Day-Lewis; yet his *Mrs Middleditch* is as accomplished, sympathetic and as truly contemporary as any poem in the book. And, if you had first come across E. E. Cummings's poem 42 (page 60) on a pop poster, with a psychedelic squiggle all round it in yellow, orange and purple, would you have guessed that the poet was born in 1894?

On the other hand, reference to the modern scene is not the only way in which a poem can show that it belongs to our own age. Ted Hughes's *Pike* contains not a single line that would not have been as true 2,000 years ago as it is today, yet it could not possibly have been written before the middle of this century. Poetry has many modes and many mansions. It can be direct or oblique, simple or complex, casual or formal, down to earth or other worldly, up to the minute or timeless. And if there is any side of life, any aspect of knowledge or experience, which is not a fit and proper subject for poetry, I have yet to find it.

NORMAN NICHOLSON

CONTENTS

xi

xii

MISSION

The wind went over
me
saying
   Why are you so distressed

Oh I said I
can't seem to make
anything
   round enough to last

But why
the wind
said
   should you be so distressed

as if anything here belonged to you
as if anything here were your concern

A. R. Ammons

BUSHMILLS

This is some
kind Gaelic
dream: nothing

can taste this
good or be
this warm

all the way
home again
and when I

think of those
fine old
Irishmen

working ten
long years
to make this

whiskey just
for me it
gives me pause.

Carroll Arnett

THE DARE

I always
ask too

much: it's
the very

least I
can do.

Carroll Arnett

NEXT

Your problem
is not my
problem, or
if it were

it would not
be yours but
mine. You see,
of course. It's

not that I
don't want to
help. I do,
of course. It's

just that I
want you to
have something
of your own.

ECONOMIC COSMOHAGIOGRAPHY

The city has no centre:
Since early this century
People went to live on the
Perimeter of the periphery.
They live two by two
In rooms ten by ten
Where the men wash the dishes
And the women watch the men.

At Hounslow and Pinner
The dwellings are clean,
The railings have
Handpolished light inbetween,
And the Faithful
Go on painting the dirt . . .

3

Even if you knocked at every house
You wouldn't find a man who could recognise a louse
Or a Saint in a hair shirt.

Michael Baldwin

WASDALE HEAD CHURCH, 1957

Here in this country churchyard
The signs are carved to stand:
The land keeps alive the living
And the dead keep alive the land.

Great beasts drop skulls on the mountain,
And there their horns take root:
The headless herds at pasture
Hide grazing necks in fruit.

Michael Baldwin

THE POSTILION HAS BEEN
STRUCK BY LIGHTNING

He was the best postilion
I ever had. That summer in Europe
Came and went
In striding thunder-rain.
His tasselled shoulders bore up
More bad days than he could count
Till he entered his last storm in the mountains,

4

You to whom a postilion
Means only a cocked hat in a museum
Or a light
Anecdote, pity this one
Burnt at milord's expense far from home
Having seen every sight
But never anyone struck by lightning.

Patricia Beer

FOUR YEARS AFTER

'The perfectly preserved body of a British mountaineer was found near Courmayeur yesterday more than four years after he fell to his death on the Géant glacier.'

Yes, this was my husband, I
Cannot say 'is' though he has
Not changed since his dying day
Four years ago. Certainly
Ice is strong as saintliness
To keep corruption away.

I have altered in these years,
Better or less rightly wed,
Uglier or handsomer
Than I was then. All my tears
Rolled, grief like cargo shifted,
Grew and was cut like my hair.

I have moved but he not once,
For fifty moons not one cell.
Look at his glassy aplomb
Which has not been splintered since
Out of death and life he fell
To nothing. I could kill him.

Patricia Beer

ARMISTICE DAY

As I was going to work that morning
I saw the flag at half mast
And remembered individual death,
A young cousin who choked, a grandfather
Who rattled all night like snoring
And several others.

I did not ask for some time
'Who?'
Being afraid to know
To hear someone's name.

It was Armistice Day
So I was finally told.

Why ever did I say: 'What a relief,
I thought somebody was dead.'
For I remember plural death
As well as singular,
The red mutilated sky over Plymouth
And in the moorland towns
The ambulance men standing by all night
And several other incidents.

Patricia Beer

ABBEY TOMB

I told them not to ring the bells
The night the Vikings came
Out of the sea and passed us by.
The fog was thick as cream
And in the abbey we stood still
As if our breath might blare
Or pulses rattle if we once
Stopped staring at the door.

Through the walls and through the fog
We heard them passing by.
The deafer monks thanked God too soon
And later only I
Could catch the sound of prowling men
Still present in the hills
So everybody else agreed
To ring the abbey bells.

And even while the final clang
Still snored upon the air,
And while the ringers joked their way
Down round the spiral stair,
Before the spit of fervent prayer
Had dried into the stone
The raiders came back through the fog
And killed us one by one.

Father Abbot at the altar
Lay back with his knees
Doubled under him, caught napping
In the act of praise.
Brother John lay unresponsive
In the warming room.
The spiders came out for the heat
And then the rats for him.

Under the level of the sheep
Who graze here all the time
We lie now, under tourists' feet
Who in good weather come.
I told them not to ring the bells
But centuries of rain
And blustering have made their tombs
Look just as right as mine.

Patricia Beer

REASONS FOR REFUSAL

Busy old lady, charitable tray
Of social emblems: poppies, people's blood—
I must refuse, make you flush pink
Perplexed by abrupt No-thank-you.
Yearly I keep up this small priggishness,
Would wince worse if I wore one.
Make me feel better, fetch a white feather, do.

Everyone has list of dead in war,
Regrets most of them, e.g.

Uncle Cyril: small boy in lace and velvet
With pushing sisters muscling all around him,
And lofty brothers, whiskers and stiff collars;
The youngest was the one who copped it.
My mother showed him to me,
Neat letters high up on the cenotaph
That wedding-caked it up above the park,
And shadowed birds on Isaac Watts' white shoulders.

And father's friends, like Sandy Vincent;
Brushed sandy hair, moustache, and staring eyes.
Kitchener claimed him, but the Southern Railway
Held back my father, made him guilty.
I hated the khaki photograph,
It left a patch on the wallpaper after I took it down.

Others I knew stick on the mind,
And Tony Lister often—
Eyes like holes in foolscap, suffered from piles,
Day after day went sick with constipation
Until they told him he could drive a truck—
Blown up with Second Troop in Greece:
We sang all night once when we were on guard.

And Ken Gee, our lance-corporal, Christian
    Scientist—
Everyone liked him, knew that he was good—
Had leg and arm blown off, then died.

Not all were good. Gross Corporal Rowlandson
Fell in the canal, the corrupt Sweet-water,
And rolled there like a log, drunk and drowned.
And I've always been glad of the death of Dick
    Benjamin,
A foxy urgent dainty ball-room dancer—
Found a new role in military necessity
As R.S.M. He waltzed out on parade
To make himself hated. Really hated, not an act,
He was a proper little porcelain sergeant-major—
The earliest bomb made smithereens:
Coincidence only, several have assured me.

In the school hall was pretty glass
Where prissy light shone through St George—
The highest holiest manhood, he!
And underneath were slain Old Boys
In tasteful lettering on whited slab—
And, each November, Ferdy the Headmaster
Reared himself squat and rolled his eyeballs upward,
Rolled the whole roll-call off an oily tongue,
Remorselessly from A to Z.

Of all the squirmers, Roger Frampton's lips
Most elegantly curled, showed most disgust.
He was a pattern of accomplishments,
And joined the Party first, and left it first,
At OCTU won a prize belt, most improbable,
Was desert-killed in '40, much too soon.

His name should burn right through that monument.

No poppy, thank you.

Martin Bell

SENILIO'S WEATHER SAW

If Church spire be clëar
Twill be däamp round here

If it be not
Twill be bloody hot

When thee caän't see spire
Church be on fire

And we'll hang parson, squire
And the whole bleeding choir.

Martin Bell

ULTIMATE ANTHOLOGY

Jacket it winsomely in primrose yellow!
Here A, B, C are drained of words they said—
Decently wild now, each a handsome fellow,
With X, and Y, and charming little Z.

Martin Bell

THE ROMANIES IN TOWN

let us leave this place, brother
it is not for us
they have built a great city
with broken glass
see how it shimmers in the evening light?

their feet are bleeding
through walking on splinters
they pretend not to notice

they have offered us a house
with cabbages in the garden
they tell us of their strange country
and want us to stay
and help them fight for it

do not listen, brother
they will bind you with promises
and with hope
on all sides stretch fields of rubble
they say we should admire the view

the young are busy building
new glass palaces
they gather up the splinters
and bathe their feet with tears

come quick come quick
we will take the road towards the sea
we will pick blackberries
from hedges in the lanes
we will pitch camp on empty moors
and watch the hawk skimming
above the trees

but if we do not fight
the hawks will die, sister
they have no time for wild birds
and will shoot us down

Anne Beresford

GUDVEIG

ᛏᚦᛌᛌ : ᛘᛂᚾ : ᚢᛆᚱᚦ · ᛘᛂᚦᚦ · ᚠᛁᚱᛁ · ᛒᛁᚱᚦ · ᛁ · ᚠᚱᚤᚾᛆ
ᛘᚤ : ᚼᛁᚠᛁ · ᛆᚱ · ᚢᚾᚦᚢᛁᚴ · ᚼᛂᛌ

Þæs: kona: uar: lagþ: firi-borð: i: grøna
lanʒ: hafi: ær: guðuih: het

This: woman: was: laid: overboard: in: Green
land's: sea: is: Gudveig: hight

So runed on a rune-stick, and the rune-stick put
In a coffin with another's body, and the coffin found
By Nörlund, in the churchyard of Herjolfsnes, and
On the ground, over the grave, was a stone
Enormous, one and a half ton, and it took
Eight men to shift it.
                            Stone there to keep down
The ghost of Gudveig: to keep quiet, keep bound
The ghost of a woman, her body overboard
Laid, in the waters around

Greenland

Francis Berry

INEXPENSIVE PROGRESS

Encase your legs in nylons,
Bestride your hills with pylons
    O age without a soul;
Away with gentle willows
And all the elmy billows
    That through your valleys roll.

Let's say good-bye to hedges
And roads with grassy edges
    And winding country lanes;
Let all things travel faster
Where motor-car is master
    Till only Speed remains.

Destroy the ancient inn-signs
But strew the roads with tin signs
    'Keep Left', 'M4', 'Keep Out!'
Command, instruction, warning,
Repetitive adorning
    The rockeried roundabout;

For every raw obscenity
Must have its small 'amenity',
    Its patch of shaven green,
And hoardings look a wonder
In banks of floribunda
    With floodlights in between.

Leave no old village standing
Which could provide a landing
    For aeroplanes to roar,
But spare such cheap defacements
As huts with shattered casements
    Unlived-in since the war.

Let no provincial High Street
Which might be your or my street
    Look as it used to do,
But let the chain stores place here
Their miles of black glass facia
    And traffic thunder through.

And if there is some scenery,
Some unpretentious greenery,

Surviving anywhere,
It does not need protecting
For soon we'll be erecting
    A Power Station there.

When all our roads are lighted
By concrete monsters sited
    Like gallows overhead,
Bathed in the yellow vomit
Each monster belches from it,
    We'll know that we are dead.

John Betjeman

HARVEST HYMN

We spray the fields and scatter
    The poison on the ground
So that no wicked wild flowers
    Upon our farm be found.
We like whatever helps us
    To line our purse with pence;
The twenty-four-hour broiler-house
    And neat electric fence.

All concrete sheds around us
    And Jaguars in the yard,
The telly lounge and deep-freeze
    Are ours from working hard.

We fire the fields for harvest,
    The hedges swell the flame,
The oak trees and the cottages
    From which our fathers came.

We give no compensation,
    The earth is ours today,
And if we lose on arable,
    Then bungalows will pay.

All concrete sheds . . . etc.

                                    John Betjeman

LINES WRITTEN TO MARTYN SKINNER
before his departure from Oxfordshire
in search of quiet— 1961

Return, return to Ealing,
    Worn poet of the farm!
Regain your boyhood feeling
    Of uninvaded calm!
For there the leafy avenues
    Of limes and chestnut mix'd
Do widely wind, by art designed,
    The costly houses 'twixt.

No early morning tractors
    The thrush and blackbird drown,
No nuclear reactors
    Bulge hideous on the down,
No youth upon his motor-bike
    His lust for power fulfils
With dentist's drill intent to kill
    The silence of the hills.

In Ealing on a Sunday
    Bell-haunted quiet falls,
In Ealing on a Monday
    'Milk-o!' the milkman calls;

No lorries grind in bottom gear
   Up steep and narrow lanes,
Nor constant here offend the ear
   Low-flying aeroplanes.

Return, return to Ealing,
   Worn poet of the farm!
Regain your boyhood feeling
   Of uninvaded calm!
Where smoothly glides the bicycle
   And softly flows the Brent
And a gentle gale from Perivale
   Sends up the hayfield scent.

John Betjeman

BY THE NINTH GREEN,
ST ENODOC

Dark of primaeval pine encircles me
With distant thunder of an angry sea
While wrack and resin scent alternately
   The air I breathe.

On slate compounded before man was made
The ocean ramparts roll their light and shade
Up to Bray Hill and, leaping to invade,
   Fall back and seethe.

A million years of unrelenting tide
Have smoothed the strata of the deep cliffside:
How long ago did rock with rock collide
   To shape these hills?

One day the mayfly's life, three weeks the cleg's,
The woodworm's four-year cycle bursts its eggs,
The flattened centipede lets loose its legs
    And stings and kills.

Hot life pulsating in this foreshore dry,
Damp life upshooting from the reed-beds high,
Under those barrows, dark against the sky,
    The Iron Age dead—

Why is it that a sunlit second sticks?
What force collects all this and seeks to fix
This fourth March morning nineteen sixty-six
    Deep in my head?

John Betjeman

CORNISH CLIFFS

Those moments, tasted once and never done,
Of long surf breaking in the mid-day sun,
A far-off blow-hole booming like a gun—

The seagulls plane and circle out of sight
Below this thirsty, thrift-encrusted height,
The veined sea-campion buds burst into white

And gorse turns tawny orange, seen beside
Pale drifts of primroses cascading wide
To where the slate falls sheer into the tide.

More than in gardened Surrey, nature spills
A wealth of heather, kidney-vetch and squills
Over these long-defended Cornish hills.

A gun-emplacement of the latest war
Looks older than the hill fort built before
Saxon or Norman headed for the shore.

And in the shadowless, unclouded glare
Deep blue above us fades to whiteness where
A misty sea-line meets the wash of air.

Nut-smell of gorse and honey-smell of ling
Waft out to sea the freshness of the spring
On sunny shallows, green and whispering.

The wideness which the lark-song gives the sky
Shrinks at the clang of sea-birds sailing by
Whose notes are tuned to days when seas are high.

From today's calm, the lane's enclosing green
Leads inland to a usual Cornish scene—
Slate cottages with sycamore between,

Small fields and tellymasts and wires and poles
With, as the everlasting ocean rolls,
Two chapels built for half a hundred souls.

John Betjeman

AGRICULTURAL CARESS

Keep me from Thelma's sister Pearl!
She puts my senses in a whirl,
Weakens my knees and keeps me waiting
Until my heart stops palpitating.

The debs may turn disdainful backs
On Pearl's uncouth mechanic slacks,
And outraged see the fire that lies
And smoulders in her long-lashed eyes.

Have they such weather-freckled features,
The smooth sophisticated creatures?
Ah, not to them such limbs belong,
Such animal movements sure and strong,

Such arms to take a man and press
In agricultural caress
His head to hers, and hold him there
Deep buried in her chestnut hair.

God shrive me from this morning lust
For supple farm girls: if you must,
Send the cold daughter of an earl—
But spare me Thelma's sister Pearl!

John Betjeman

THE EDUCATORS

In their
limousines the
teachers come: by
hundreds. O the
square is
blackened with dark suits, with grave
scholastic faces. They
wait to be summoned.
                    These are the
educators, the
father-figures. O you could

warm with love for the firm lips, the
responsible foreheads. Their
ties are strongly set, between their collars. They
pass with dignity the exasperation of waiting.

A
bell rings. They turn. On the
wide steps my
dwarf is standing, both hands raised. He
cackles with laughter. Welcome, he cries, welcome
to our elaborate Palace. It is indeed. He
is tumbling in cartwheels over the steps. The
teachers turn to each other their grave faces.

With
a single grab they have him up by the shoulders. They
dismantle him. Limbs, O
limbs and delicate organs, limbs and
guts, eyes, the tongue, the
lobes of the brain, glands; tonsils, several
eyes, limbs, the tongue,
a kidney, pants, livers, more
kidneys, limbs, the tongue
pass from hand to hand, in their serious hands. He is
utterly gone. Wide
crumbling steps.

They
return to their cars. They
drive off smoothly, without disorder;
watching the road.

D. M. Black

HOME, HOME ON THE RANGE

Reading today of another man roasted alive,
I conclude that space-trips are a dangerous game;
But even if some chap does reach a star,
He'll come home, if he does, to much the same
Mayhem and trickery and paranoia.
They'll have the bunting out when he returns;
The journalists will ramp, the crowds will roar,
And even Presidents give pause to praise
The Moon-Man—from their rapport with murder.
Though astronauts are not articulate,
Will he find it strange, after that lunar quiet
To sense once more the lineaments of hate
On every human face, and hear that riot?
I think of those disciples who once saw
Upon a mountain top the transfigured Christ
And, having seen him, stumbled down to meet
A lunatic boy on whom their skill was lost,
And wonder if the Moon-Man also will,
After his stellar journey pause and think,
'The capsule that bore me could bear the bomb',
Or dazed by the applause just stammer out,
'God bless America, and God bless Mom!'

Thomas Blackburn

DEATH OF A WHALE

When the mouse died, there was a sort of pity:
the tiny, delicate creature made for grief.
Yesterday, instead, the dead whale on the reef
drew an excited multitude to the jetty.
How must a whale die to wring a tear?
Lugubrious death of a whale: the big

feast for the gulls and sharks; the tug
of the tide simulating life still there,
until the air, polluted, swings this way
like a door ajar from a slaughterhouse.
Pooh! pooh! spare us, give us the death of a mouse
by its tiny hole; not this in our lovely bay.
—Sorry, we are, too, when a child dies;
but at the immolation of a race, who cries?

John Blight

OCTOBER SILENCE

If gardens into slavery are sold
Not by dark rustlings in the slightest fold
But, stripped and palsied, drugged and unaware,
Are duly by their own bright hush laid bare,
Portent of that deceiving hour most fair
When, opulently neither young nor old,
The frailest rose may seem a thrust too bold,
    Almost a passion is this doveless air,
    And undertone of spring not quite retold.

Undisguised, an open show of gold,
Her honied breath at noon the most controlled
Of all the winds that gently now prepare,
Silence advances, intrigues everywhere,
Smiling but softer if her deepened care
For loosening petals that must still withhold
Suggests a client impotent and cold—
    When just as lusty now as ever he were
    The sun comes fawning to the bed of mould.

Frederick Bock

ON SEEING VOSKHOD OVER
EDINBURGH

On a cold October night
Edinburgh's sky was punctuated,
Not by a divine presence,
But by the stabbing cigarette-end-like apparition
Of three men in a spaceship.
I looked out from my house
In a hundred-year-old tenement
And felt that Komarov, Yegerov, and Feoktistov
Were fellow travellers of mine.
For it's a long way from Zazakhstan to Scotland
And it's a long way my home is from Voskhod.
Yet I saw
The stabbing cigarette-end-like shape,
I watched as the red light flashed
Across the sky.
For four minutes we Scots saw
The scientific age in action.
And as we retreated back into our tenements
And thought once more of slums,
We also saw that an alternative exists.

Alan Bold

5 WAYS TO KILL A MAN

There are many cumbersome ways to kill a man:
you can make him carry a plank of wood
to the top of a hill and nail him to it. To do this
properly you require a crowd of people
wearing sandals, a cock that crows, a cloak
to dissect, a sponge, some vinegar and one
man to hammer the nails home.

Or you can take a length of steel,
shaped and chased in a traditional way,
and attempt to pierce the metal cage he wears.
But for this you need white horses,
English trees, men with bows and arrows,
at least two flags, a prince and a
castle to hold your banquet in.

Dispensing with nobility, you may, if the wind
allows, blow gas at him. But then you need
a mile of mud sliced through with ditches,
not to mention black boots, bomb craters,
more mud, a plague of rats, a dozen songs
and some round hats made of steel.

In an age of aeroplanes, you may fly
miles above your victim and dispose of him by
pressing one small switch. All you then
require is an ocean to separate you, two
systems of government, a nation's scientists,
several factories, a psychopath and
land that no one needs for several years.

These are, as I began, cumbersome ways
to kill a man. Simpler, direct, and much more neat
is to see that he is living somewhere in the middle
of the twentieth century, and leave him there.

Edwin Brock

ON BEING CHOSEN FOR A SCHOOLS ANTHOLOGY

Mostly shame, I suppose, at inadequacies
explained away: the right rhyme chosen
for the wrong reason. And tiptoed voices
nibbling at a line which once was fact.

My own two kids could tell them: the slapped
face and the breakfast roar of the bore who sat
cuddling himself in the flat's best corner.

If the truth were known, it is nothing I have
written should be shown in a cloth book in a
cold classroom. But myself in a desk I have
not outgrown with the innocents ringed
around me—pausing as I put in my thumb,
exclaiming as I drew a plum, applauding as I make
the private joke I have in time become.

Edwin Brock

SYMBOLS OF THE SIXTIES

On a quiet Sunday
when the sun is out
you can drive to
a village in Kent
which boasts a
coffee bar with plastic
tables. Among the
paraphernalia on the
walls a bird in a
painted cage says
Ban the bomb ban
the bomb ban the
bomb ban the bomb.
Boys in plastic jackets
fidget there with
beehive girls. The chickens
look brittle and taste
as though they were made
in the same factory
as the tabletops.

Edwin Brock

A MOMENT OF RESPECT

Two things I remember about my grandfather:
his threadbare trousers, and the way he adjusted
his half-hunter watch two minutes every day.

When I asked him why he needed to know the time so
exactly, he said a business man could lose a fortune
by being two minutes late for an appointment.

When he died he left two meerschaum pipes
and a golden sovereign on a chain. Somebody
threw the meerschaum pipes away, and
there was an argument about the sovereign.

On the day of his burial the church clock chimed
as he was lowered down into the clay, and all
the family advanced their watches by two minutes.

Edwin Brock

RICHNESS

There is speed and stress and richness here for the eye,
Beauty everywhere, bold and strongly striding,
Clouds tumbling, teeming, in trouble of sky,
Hugely wind-herded, riding and over-riding:
White in the West, mainward, the galleons rising,
With pressure, constancy, and pride of sailing,
Breasted, abounding, will stay for no man's hailing,
Wind-colts, wanton in this their exercising.

So welkin-world waxes, and as the skies
Cumber, discumber, green grass-glory lies,

Ravin'd about one, rolling, a sunlight, a sea,
Wave in the wind-rush silken—and, light as love,
A glitter of lantern-leaves is gold above,
Gathering spread sky-scurry all to one tree!

Arthur J. Bull

LEAVES

Do not be melancholy for the leaves,
There is no fever in them, in their blood
No hectic rages; they are understood,
Accepted, by the earth, and from the tree;
Our folly, not their perishing, deceives,
And there is calm throughout the dying wood.

Nor is it weakness only when they fall,
The leaf is thrust by action from the tree,
Its launching, though a death, deliberate:
There is a purpose that we cannot see,
And we lose heart too soon, not knowing all,
And fear, not understanding how to wait.

Renewal stirs, how richly, in the mould:
The sacred chemistry of change goes on,
Birds in the fallen carpeting are bold,
And the praiseworthy worm, though silently,
Does not neglect the duty to be done,
Among the nourishing, the lavish gold.

Sometimes, in our mild winter, you will see,
The oak, or sycamore, still scarecrow clad,
When March comes round, with shreds of pauperdom,

Brown ragged remnant of the valiancy,
That mustered once to make a season glad,
And you will praise this courage in the tree,
As if it would not, like yourself, make room.

Arthur J. Bull

NATURE

Do not be taken in
By grace of water, smile of sky:
We are beleaguered garrison,
And it is time we buy.

Our foes are myriadminded—
Bees like dragons hum,
Wasps are tigers of the air,
Spider sits plotting in her lair
How to achieve a general doom,
Weave in one universal web
Our cities proud and palaces.

Seas wash our bones from kindly air
Into the deep thalassic cave,
And every upland tarn extends a fair
Smooth invitation to the grave;
Under the shining water lies
A house from which no bride may rise.

Nature's the ancient enemy
No man of war can put to flight,
And that dark line of green you see
Is creeping on you in the night:
No-one may contract out of this
Embrace and marriage of the abyss.

Arthur J. Bull

THE WIND

After these long still days of frost and fire
The sun destructive glowing his desire,
After the ringing iron on the road,
The January sky's impending load,
After the snow impertinently thrown
On rich and poor; the long surcease of noise,
Then, broken by the running streams alone,
A meretricious thaw, that troubles boys—
After all this, it is not ill to wake,
And hear the redskin wind about the stake,
Howling, and from your bedroom eyrie know,
World-currents have, so late, begun to blow:
That, cradled in the parish, you can share
An ocean-travelling, unmastered air;
That you can range, and O, rejoice with it
Beyond the grasp of iron winter's wit!

Wind is the present, and regrets no past,
Tears down the rigid house of winter's waste;
Wind in the metaphysic of the sky,
Omnipotently puts negation by:
I hear its call, Come out and celebrate
The living year. Wind opens winter's gate.
I hear it raging in the pines, and see
The poplar bend, that vext, that female tree;
I hear it, knowing in the dawn of day,
This turmoil comes a long Atlantic way.
It is importunate, and takes no keep,
Of watching misery, or windowed sleep;
Lets our close-printed page of passion be,
Offers no commentary; wind is free.
And yet with giant hand it breaks the bar,
That held me in, and lets me travel far:
Out of this day, and yesterday, I go,
Into the fairest region time can show,

And, for this moment, absolutely live,
In what will never be, time's fugitive.
Need I be troubled, borne on such a wing,
The last great wind of Winter, first of Spring?

Arthur J. Bull

AND HERE I AM,
FIGHTING DANDELIONS

It's not their bright yellow
more frank than boastful.

Yet, though hurried and harried
careering and careening
I fare forth
to cut down dandelions.

I patrol the lawn, resenting how they spread
like a foreign policy.

At times I catch one *in flagrante delicto*
(in fragrant delight?)
in an orgy of miscegenation with a bee,
without benefit of clergy.

I dig up dandelions
at the height of their excesses.

(I fight fair.
No chemicals.
I'm a Rachel Carson man
and Organic Gardening—
and damn the fluoridation racket.)

Word goes forth:
'Burke's after us.
Hurry, proliferate,
be a population explosion.'

From away back
the nice old lady next door
friendly to all
yet hypnotized by the *mores*

She raged against the Eyetalians
who swept across the grass in springtime
harvesting the honest dandelion

She fumed because they dug holes in her lawn—
or was she but responding
to the way they crouched at their work
(stoop labour)
and hurried like stage criminals,
disappearing around the corner of Friendship Avenue?

Kenneth Burke

HEAVY, HEAVY—WHAT HANGS OVER?

At eighty
reading lines
he wrote at twenty

The storm now past

A gust in the big tree
splatters raindrops
on the roof

Kenneth Burke

ECONOMICS

Menelaus
    Personally I never cared for the girl:
    She wasn't really very much to look at
    At close quarters. Many of us
    Had seen better in Corinth, let alone Naucratis
        ... What?
    Naturally pride came into it: the family feud
    Was taken seriously ... but most of all
    The Trojan corn monopoly, you understand ... the
        Bosporus blockade—

    Our Black Sea trade
    Was quite extensive, and a small country like
        Attica
    With no internal resources at all
    Depends to a very large extent
    On imports coming via the Dardanelles
    It meant something in those days. As to Helen—
    Well, she provided a convenient rallying cry
    (Our propagandists did extremely well
    With their material). But I must point out
    The Trojan War was quite a serious business.

Miles Burrows

ODYSSEUS

'It was no Hellenic cruise, I can tell
You that much. What with men overboard;
Running before a broken sea;
Fogs; tides; landing in a surf;
Various collisions; difficulties

Of fixing our position; wrecks;
And me having to organize it all,
With victualling routines and messing duties.
The question of stowage: vegetables, wine,
The extra issues on exceptional occasions,
After severe exposure, or heavy work.
Or there'd be doldrums: not a cat's paw of wind
In the Aegean; keep the crew occupied
Whipping the rope-ends. It wasn't child's play.
Then we'd break from moorings, the ship awash,
Ropes parting, human flotsam
Adding to the beauties of the Aegean.
Righting a weather lurch, keeping her head up
Close to a freshening wind, making for dead
    water.
The half-hearted ineptitudes of the crew earning
Contempt, not laughter.
                    She was a fine ship, though,
Clinker-built pine, though she made some water
Before the end. But how to keep your temper
With a lounging crew, no sense of discipline,
No muscles? How to explain the necessity
Of keeping fit, to men who look with pigs' eyes,
Show no sign of respect, have a faulty grasp
On the oar? How to explain the elementary
    precautions:
Unshipping the rudder before landing, don't let
    her
Turn broadside on to a heavy surf?
Still, it was better than earning a livelihood
Scratching up goat dirt on an Ithacan
    smallholding.'

Miles Burrows

33

TROY

Ashes of luxury float over a dead city
Figments shimmer among white fragments
The flames are pallid in the sun's light
A hot wind blows over dry corn.
A lot of corn was damaged that year
A considerable part of the Black Sea harvest
Had to be written off altogether
As a dead loss. Which is all that could be expected.

The besieging army had been living richly off the crops
Of the outlying cornfields for the past ten years.
When they penetrated the citadel, they found the
    granaries
Practically empty, their totality expended.
The besieged statisticians had been calculating rather
    carefully
(It's their job, of course,) for a ten-year duration.
Then the troops began the extermination
Of the entire populace both military and civilian
(With the normal exceptions made in cases
Of exceptional good looks, or, more rarely,
Plausible offers of exceptional ransom-money):
Atrocities were committed, that goes without saying;
The screams of the mutilated would certainly have wrung
    tears
From less experienced personnel. But as it was
In spite of the stringent injunctions to restraint
Laid upon us by our senior officers
Things took their customary course. Women and children
It is generally recognized in military quarters
Are the fair game of a victorious army.
But after the first wave of shock-troops had gone in
And the second followed, the Thracians, I believe,
And the third, the Phrygians, followed closely
By Thebans, Illyrians, Corfiots and Euboeians,

The Attican contingent came about thirtieth.
There was already a slight feeling of anti-climax
Unavoidable after a ten-year tension;
Then to arrive in a deserted city, greeted only
By corpses already dismembered, and the ironic
      encouragement
Of those who had arrived on the scene much earlier.
The forces of cohesion, the *esprit de corps*
Never at the best of times strong between Greek
      municipalities,
Having worn extremely thin in the course of the ten years
Gave way altogether. It was about then
That they turned to desecrating the local cathedrals
In a mood less of avarice than of pique, and a feeling
Of having been deprived of their due of destruction.

As for the alleged storm, which many old campaigners
Will still tell you occurred supernaturally
When the Greek armies were sailing back home again
(As if they were in any hurry to re-greet their wives,
And could not afford to wait for more clement weather)
The 'Storm', and the heavy loss of ships and men,
Was a tempest of ill tempers, of disappointments,
Of envy and disillusion. That was the malignant disaster
Which turned on the Greek army on their return voyage
And did such harm to morale and discipline
As to reduce the numbers of the victorious army
Very considerably. And even now
Most of the survivors are ashamed to speak of it.
(By and large, of course, the survivors
Were those who had played the least creditable part.)

Miles Burrows

A FROSTY NIGHT

All night the constellations sang
there, in that perfect church, and rang
in the cold belfry of the night,
strewing their splintered light
over the bare sea and the humpbacked fields,
while the hammer of frost, that kills
a flower and leaves a feather
on the gatepost, swung from the weather.

All the lanes grooved round the hillsides
shrank; a brittle skin grew over the puddles;
a sharp wind sawed at the birches,
and the sleeping trunks and branches,
cracking their bark and their frozen flesh,
groaned out of a leafless peace,
and the catkins hung limp in the cruel air
where they had danced the day before.

In the clear morning a salt of frost,
flung down thickly by the moon's ghost,
lay on the roofs and the sloping grass
of the rough hills, sparkling like glass.
And like a warm beast in a shippen
the animal body of the sun
was struggling up, and with stiff knees
heaved itself out of the trees.

Philip Callow

MONDAY SNOWFALL

Look up, and it's a fast swirl of breadcrumbs,
a storm of dirt turning us all dizzy,
a plague of locusts eating up the colour—

and that really happened, in just twenty minutes.
We stand by the glass, watching single snowflakes,
how the soft stars dance about like feathers;
then at night walk out, find that everything's freezing,
mince along like ladies on the slippery pavement.
I catch a workmen's bus and get home muttering
'Monday's no time to enjoy winter landscapes.'

Philip Callow

BY ST THOMAS WATER

By St Thomas Water
Where the river is thin
We look for a jam-jar
To catch the quick fish in.
Through St Thomas Church-yard
Jessie and I ran
The day we took the jam-pot
Off the dead man.

On the scuffed tombstone
The grey flowers fell,
Cracked was the water,
Silent the shell.
The snake for an emblem
Swirled on the slab,
Across the beach of sky the sun
Crawled like a crab.

'If we walk,' said Jessie,
'Seven times round,
We shall hear a dead man
Speaking underground.'
Round the stone we danced, we sang,

Watched the sun drop,
Laid our hearts and listened
At the tomb-top.

Soft as the thunder
At the storm's start
I heard a voice as clear as blood,
Strong as the heart.
But what words were spoken
I can never say,
I shut my fingers round my head,
Drove them away.

'What are those letters, Jessie,
Cut so sharp and trim
All round this holy stone
With earth up to the brim?'
Jessie traced the letters
Black as coffin-lead.
'He is not dead but sleeping,'
Slowly she said.

I looked at Jessie,
Jessie looked at me,
And our eyes in wonder
Grew wide as the sea.
Past the green and bending stones
We fled hand in hand,
Silent through the tongues of grass
To the river strand.

By the creaking cypress
We moved as soft as smoke
For fear all the people
Underneath awoke.
Over all the sleepers
We darted light as snow

In case they opened up their eyes,
Called us from below.

Many a day has faltered
Into many a year
Since the dead awoke and spoke
And we would not hear.
Waiting in the cold grass
Under a crinkled bough,
Quiet stone, cautious stone,
What do you tell me now?

Charles Causley

RESERVOIR STREET

In nineteen twenty-six, the year
Of the Strike, on a day of bubbling heat
I went to stay with my sun-faced cousins
Who lived in a house on Reservoir Street.

Auntie stood strong as the Eddystone Lighthouse.
A terrible light shone out of her head.
Her children scuttled like ships for harbour.
You must let them know what's what, she said.

Her five prime-beef boys circled round me.
They didn't enjoy what they saw at all.
We couldn't make any more of each other
Than the map of stains on the bedroom wall.

All night long on the road to the city
The motor-car tyres rubbed out the dark.
Early in the morning I watched from the window
The sun like a killer come out of the park.

Down in the reservoir I saw a man drowning.
His flooding head came over the side.
They poked him out of a parcel of water.
He's poisoned the drink! my cousins cried.

I packed my bag and I said to Auntie,
I think I'll go home on the one o'clock train.
My, they all said, he wants his mammy.
They never let me forget it again.

Through the Cornish jungle-country
Like a parrot the train screamed home.
I thought of my brother who slept beside me,
Four walls round us pure as cloam.

When I got to the house my head was thunder.
The bed lay open as a shell.
Sweet was my brother's kiss, and sweeter
The innocent water from the well.

Charles Causley

SCHOOL AT FOUR O'CLOCK

At four o'clock the building enters harbour.
All day it seems that we have been at sea.
Now, having lurched through the last of the water,
We lie, stone-safe, beside the jumping quay.
The stiff waves propped against the classroom window,
The razor-back of cliffs we never pass,
The question-mark of green coiling behind us,
Have all turned into cabbages, slates, grass.

Up the slow hill a squabble of children wanders
As silence dries the valley like a drought,
When suddenly that speechless cry is raging
Once more round these four walls to be let out.
Like playing cards the Delabole slates flutter,
The founding stone is shaken in its mine,
The faultless evening light begins to stutter
As the cry hurtles down the chimney-spine.

Packing my bag with useless bits of paper
I wonder, when the last word has been said,
If I'd prefer to find each sound was thudding
Not round the school, but just inside my head.
I watch where the street lamp with sodium finger
Touches the darkening voices as they fall.
Outside? Inside? Perhaps either condition's
Better than his who hears nothing at all.

And I recall another voice. A teacher
Long years ago, saying, *I think I know
Where all the children come from, but the puzzle
To me is, as they grow up, where they go?*
Love, wonder, marvellous hope. All these can wither
With crawling years like flowers on a stalk;
Or, to some Piper's tune, vanish for ever
As creatures murdered on a morning walk.

Though men may blow this building up with powder,
Drag its stone guts to knacker's yard, or tip,
Smash its huge heart to dust, and spread the shingle
By the strong sea, or sink it like a ship—
Listen. Through the clear shell of air the voices
Still strike like water from the mountain bed;
The cry of those who to a certain valley
Hungry and innocent came. And were not fed.

Charles Causley

41

DEATH OF A POET

Suddenly his mouth filled with sand.
His tractor of blood stopped thumping.
He held five icicles in each hand.
His heart packed up jumping.

His face turned the colour of something forgotten in the
    larder.
His thirty-two teeth were expelled on the kitchen floor.
His muscles, at long last, got considerably harder.
He felt younger than he had for some time before.

Four heroes, steady as wrestlers, each carried him on a
    shoulder
Into a great grey church laid out like a brain.
An iron bowl sent out stiff rays of chrysanthemums. It
    grew colder.
The sun, as expected, failed to break through the pane.

The parson boomed like a dockyard gun at a christening.
Somebody read from the bible. It seemed hours.
I got the feeling you were curled up inside the box,
    listening.
There was the thud of hymn-books, the stench of flowers.

I remembered hearing your voice on a bloody foment
Of Atlantic waters. The words burned clear as a flare.
Life begins, you said, as of this moment.
A bird flew down out of the hurling air.

Over the church a bell broke like a wave upended.
The hearse left for winter with a lingering hiss.
I looked in the wet sky for a sign, but no bird descended.
I went across the road to the pub; wrote this.

Charles Causley

LORD SYCAMORE

I climbed Lord Sycamore's Castle,
The wind was blowing red.
'Top of the morning, my lord,' I cried.
'Top to you,' he said.

'Welcome to Sycamore Castle,'
His smile as sharp as tin,
'Where many broken men come out
That in one piece go in.'

With pusser's eggs and bacon
My belly it was rare.
'Together,' said Lord Sycamore,
'Let's take the dancing air.'

With a running finger
He chucked me under the chin.
Felt with a lover's quiet hand
Where he might best begin.

Suddenly he cooled me
As we laughed and joked.
Although the month was May, my breath
On the morning smoked.

On the sum of my body
Lord Sycamore got to work,
Pulled the answer like a rose
Out of my mouth with a jerk.

On Lord Sycamore's Castle
I heard the morning stop;
Over my head, the springing birds,
Under my feet, the drop.

Charles Causley

pusser's: strictly naval; naval issue.

BALLAD OF THE BREAD MAN

Mary stood in the kitchen
Baking a loaf of bread.
An angel flew in through the window.
We've a job for you, he said.

God in his big gold heaven,
Sitting in his big blue chair,
Wanted a mother for his little son.
Suddenly saw you there.

Mary shook and trembled,
It isn't true what you say.
Don't say that, said the angel.
The baby's on its way.

Joseph was in the workshop
Planing a piece of wood.
The old man's past it, the neighbours said.
That girl's been up to no good.

And who was that elegant fellow,
They said, in the shiny gear?
The things they said about Gabriel
Were hardly fit to hear.

Mary never answered,
Mary never replied.
She kept the information,
Like the baby, safe inside.

It was election winter.
They went to vote in town.
When Mary found her time had come
The hotels let her down.

The baby was born in an annex
Next to the local pub.
At midnight, a delegation
Turned up from the Farmers' Club.

They talked about an explosion
That made a hole in the sky,
Said they'd been sent to the Lamb & Flag
To see God come down from on high.

A few days later a bishop
And a five-star general were seen
With the head of an African country
In a bullet-proof limousine.

We've come, they said, with tokens
For the little boy to choose.
Told the tale about war and peace
In the television news.

After them came the soldiers
With rifle and bomb and gun,
Looking for enemies of the state.
The family had packed and gone.

When they got back to the village
The neighbours said, to a man,
That boy will never be one of us,
Though he does what he blessed well can.

He went round to all the people
A paper crown on his head.
Here is some bread from my father.
Take, eat, he said.

Nobody seemed very hungry.
Nobody seemed to care.
Nobody saw the god in himself
Quietly standing there.

He finished up in the papers.
He came to a very bad end.
He was charged with bringing the living to life.
No man was that prisoner's friend.

There's only one kind of punishment
To fit that kind of a crime.
They rigged a trial and shot him dead.
They were only just in time.

They lifted the young man by the leg,
They lifted him by the arm,
They locked him in a cathedral
In case he came to harm.

They stored him safe as water
Under seven rocks.
One Sunday morning he burst out
Like a jack-in-the-box.

Through the town he went walking.
He showed them the holes in his head.
Now do you want any loaves? he cried.
Not today, they said.

Charles Causley

IMMUNITY

Lining up with the naked sailors,
The smell of Africa blown off-shore,
I watched the sweat run down to my ankles,
Borrowed a tickler from the man next door.

The sick-bay tiffy looked more like a doctor.
The quack was nervous, his face of bread;
He might have been last man in for England,
The sky gone dark and pitch turned red.

It's nothing, he said as he dipped the needle,
Pumped it full of jungle juice.
Don't look at the man in front, that's the secret.
It's not like putting your head through a noose.

We stuck out our arms. He looked at his needle,
Showed the usual pusser's restraint,
Suddenly swallowed his oath to Hippocrates,
Fell on the deck in a number-one faint.

No one issued with a jab at Freetown.
No one complained of feeling crook.
Malaria, yellow and blackwater fever
Lay down low till we pulled up the hook.

Rocked on the antiseptic ocean
Nobody noticed the turning screw.
This would cost a fortune, we said, in peace-time,
The sun so yellow and the sea so blue.

And, for the record, off Kos a month later
Where Hippocrates lived out his term,
Most of them died of wounds or sea-water,
Including the doctor. None of a germ.

Charles Causley

tickler: cigarette made from duty-free tobacco.
sick-bay tiffy: sick-berth attendant.
quack: ship's medical officer.

GUY FAWKES' DAY

I am the caught, the crooked, the candled man
With flames for fingers and whose thin eyes fountain,
I send on the stiff air my shooting stare
And at my shoulder bear the burning mountain.

I open on the dark my wound of speeches,
With stabs, with stars its seven last words wear,
My tongue of torches with the salamander
Breeds conversaziones of despair.

Milled in the minted light my skin of silver
Now curls, now kindles on the thicket's bone.
And fired with flesh in sepulchres of slumber
Walks the white night with sparks and showers sown.

At my fixed feet soldiers my coat of carbon
Slit with the speared sky. Their sacked eyes scan
My mask of medals. In bright mirrors of breath
Our faces fuse in death. My name is man.

Charles Causley

GRAVE BY THE SEA

By the crunching, Cornish sea
Walk the man and walk the lover,
Innocent as fish that fare
In the high and hooking air,
And their deaths discover.

Beneath, you said, this turning tree,
With granite eye and stare of sand,
His heart as candid as the clay,
A seaman from the stropping bay
Took to the land.

Once this calmed, crystal hand was free
And rang the changes of the heart:
Love, like his life, a world wherein
The white-worm sin wandered not in.
Death played no part.

Wreathed, and with ringing fingers he
Passed like a prince upon the day
And from its four and twenty towers
Shot with his shaft the haggard hours,
Hauled them away.

So he set from the shaken quay
His foot upon the ocean floor
And from the wanting water's teeth
The ice-faced gods above, beneath,
Spat him ashore.

Now in the speaking of the sea
He waits under this written stone,
And kneeling at his freezing frame
I scrub my eye to see his name

And read my own.

Charles Causley

THE LAST FREEDOM

The blind man, when the skylark shakes
Trill over trill from the blue above,
Stares upward and from darkness wakes
Through sockets eloquent with love.

If our defective senses thus
Kindle at glories half-divined,
What of the joy awaiting us
When death brings freedom to the mind?

Richard Church

THE RECOGNITION

At once I recognized him; for I saw
Blood clotted in his palms, and on his shirt
Above the ribs. His foot arched like a claw
When it approached the ground, and in the dirt
A spoor of blood stigmatized Camberwell.
I traced the agony to Peckham Rye
Past parish church and Town Hall. I could tell
That by the School of Art he paused, but why
I could not understand. He may have hoped
To find a healing symbol there. He failed.
The trail of blood betrayed him as he groped
Onward from London while the darkness paled
Slowly before him, veiling as he went,
His throne and resurrection over Kent.

Richard Church

THE CAMEL

Study the camel, who has learned to wait
Impassive under load piled upon load,
Then kicked, told to un-kneel, and tread no-road
Out of the blessed shade of palm and date
Across the desert and the herbless state
Where nothing may be reaped, and nothing sowed,
His only nourishment the prodding goad,
Beneath the sun's intensity of hate.

But he is obstinate, he foots the sand
Slowly, rhythmically, day by day,
Ignoring admonition and the rod.
Wisdom we humans cannot understand
Curves his ironic lip. In his own way
He knows the hidden hundredth name for God.

Richard Church

A STRONG WIND

All day a strong wind blew
Across the green and brown from Kerry.
The leaves hurrying, two
By three, over the road, collected
In chattering groups. New berry
Dipped with old branch. Careful insects
Flew low behind their hedges.
Held back by her pretty petticoat,
Butterfly struggled. A bit of
Paper, on which a schoolgirl had written
'Máire loves Jimmy', jumped up
Into a tree. Tapping in haste,
The wind was telegraphing, hundreds
Of miles. All Ireland raced.

Austin Clarke

MEDICAL MISSIONARY OF MARY

One blowy morning, Sister Michael,
A student of midwifery,
Fell, handlebarring from her cycle,
Her habit twisted around a pedal:
She suffered bruises on her riff,
Serious injury to the spine
And so, in hope of miracle,
Was brought, a stretcher case, to Lourdes
Out of the blue, above the shrining
Of snowy peaks: unchosen, uncured
Although she had made novena, kissed
The relics: worse than ever, came back
By London, lying on her back,
Saw there, thank Heaven, a specialist
And now is on the recovery list.

Austin Clarke

UNDER CREAG MHOR

A lizard fidgets in the sun
That stuns it. Inchlong
And perfect, agile among
Pebbles, it purls its reflection

In crinkling pools. Neither
Freak nor fossil but something
Of each, legends clang
In its speck of a brain, roar

It down at no notice through brown
Peat juice, through mire
Of yellow bogland to where
It discovers its origin.

The bracken scurrs of Creag Mhor,
Pleated with clear water,
No longer house dinosaur
And plated myth. But far

Down, in the cool bright
Element of lizard's tiny
Being, in its ancient eye,
Such monsters huddle yet.

Stewart Conn

BOWLING GREEN, TROON

Not on beach-heads in an appalling light
   Do they wage war now, struck dumb
By the devouring sun—but on squares
   Of green, and with true decorum.

Woods curve and knock. Boaters
   Tilt. Beyond formal trellising children
Turn cartwheels on white sand.
   The lobster-backed sea swills out, then

In again. Rinks settled, old
   Songs are sung; medals gleam; rugs
Are spread on the grass; rough
   Cider sparkles, spilling from stone jugs.

But Willum, ancient sentry, still
   Stands staring out to sea. The numb
Wind making frills of his hair,
   He waits for Armadas that will never come.

Stewart Conn

SUMMER FARM

The sun drills the shire through and through
Till the farm is a furnace, the yard
A quivering wickerwork of flame. Pitchforks
Flash and fall. Bales are fiery ingots.
Straws sputter like squibs. Stones
Explode. From the byre, smack on time,
Old Martha comes clattering out
With buttered bannocks and milk in a pail.

Todd, his face ablaze, swims back
In what shadow there is. Hugh and John
Stretch out among sheaves. Hens squabble
For crusts; a dog flicks its tail
At a cleg; blueflies bunch like grapes.
Still the sun beats down, a hammer
On tin. And high overhead vapour-trails
Drift seaward, out past Ailsa Craig . . .

Stewart Conn

FLIGHT

Leaving the town behind, and the spoiled
  Fields, we made slowly for the hills.
    Our clothes were in rags, our
  Bodies lit with sores. Every
So often we had to water the horse.

Our farm-cart was heaped with straw. Under
    That, the real cargo.
  The soldiers scoffed. After
Searching us, though, they let us through.

We dared not stop, or look round.
  But from the side of the cart
    Came a steady trickle of blood,
Where the most drunken of the guards
  Had run his sword in among the straw.

Stewart Conn

THE ORCHARD

Loose-rigged, the orchard pitches
Like a sailing-ship caught on the swell
Of slapdash southern seas. Cargoes burst
In the hold, under canvas or barrel

On barrel piled high. And the sun
Is the colour of straw; and the sky,
Yanked brutally in, leaves heaps
Of apples rotting where they lie.

A drugged light swills the poop. Trees,
Mast and yard-arm, take the strain.
Air's bruised. Rain litters the yellow
Deck, then swabs it clear again.

Crushed branch, made flashing bowsprit,
Slithers under. Mashed shapes shoot
Through spindrift. Crude as Caliban,
Pigs stuff their filthy bellies and root

For more. Yet I remember
A simpler order in this place:
When boys in azure tunics climbed
Flimsy ladders and stepped out into space.

Stewart Conn

ABOVE PENMAENMAWR

The upland farmers have all gone;
the lane they laid twists without purpose,
visiting broken gates and overgrown
gardens, to end in clumps of gorse.

Their unroofed houses, and fallen barns,
rich in nettles, lie dead in hiding
from the wind that howls off Talyfan's
saw-tooth ridge; their walls divide

bracken from bracken; their little church
of bare rock has outlasted use:
hikers' signatures in the porch,
'Keys obtainable at the Guesthouse'.

Yet, not to sentimentalize,
their faces turned from drudgery
when the chance showed itself. There is
hardly a sign of the husbandry

of even the last to leave—so slight
was their acceptance by the land.
They left for the seaside towns, to get
easier jobs, and cash in hand.

Five miles of uplands, and beyond—
a thousand feet below—the coast,
its bright lights twinkling, freezing wind
dragging the cloud down like a frost

from Talyfan. Alone upon
these darkening, silent heights, my fears
stay stubbornly with the farmers, gone
after six hundred thankless years.

Tony Connor

DRUID'S CIRCLE

The few squat leaning rocks in a loose ring
are a disappointment to all that climb
the mountain track to see them. They are nothing
like Auschwitz, Belsen, or Buchenwald. No crime

against humanity lingers in the air
of this place. The so-called 'Sacrificial
Stone' is a boring flat expanse, bare
of any hint of blood. It doesn't look especial

in the least—except for the roughly scratched
initials: a confused palimpsest
of clumsy letters cross-hatched
on its surface. To most people the trip's a waste

of time, and, if the women shudder,
the men light pipes, the children fret,
it is the wild-eyed ba-ba and scatter
of all that moving mutton, the sight

of so much horizon, and the air,
appalling in its emptiness,
that makes them loath to explore further,
and sends them townwards, laughing with distress.

Tony Connor

ELEGY FOR ALFRED HUBBARD

Hubbard is dead, the old plumber;
who will mend our burst pipes now,
the tap that has dripped all the summer,
testing the sink's overflow?

No other like him. Young men with knowledge
of new techniques, theories from books,
may better his work straight from college,
but who will challenge his squint-eyed looks

in kitchen, bathroom, under floorboards,
rules of thumb which were often wrong;
seek as erringly stopcocks in cupboards,
or make a job last half as long?

He was a man who knew the ginnels,
alleyways, streets,—the whole district;
family secrets, minor annals,
time-honoured fictions fused to fact.

Seventy years of gossip muttered
under his cap, his tufty thatch,
so that his talk was slow and clotted,
hard to follow, and too much.

As though nothing fell, none vanished,
and time were the maze of Cheetham Hill,
in which the dead,—with jobs unfinished—,
waited to hear him ring the bell.

For much he never got round to doing,
but meant to, when the weather bucked up,
or worsened, or when his pipe was drawing,
or when he'd finished this cup.

I thought time, he forgot so often,
had forgotten him, but here's Death's pomp
over his house, and by the coffin
the son who will inherit his blowlamp,

tools, workshop, cart, and cornet,
(pride of Cheetham Prize Brass Band),—
and there's his mourning widow, Janet,
stood at the gate he'd promised to mend.

Soon he will make his final journey;
shaved and silent, strangly trim,
with never a pause to talk to any-
body: how arrow-like, for him!

In St Mark's Church,—whose dismal tower
he pointed and painted when a lad—,
they will sing his praises amidst flowers,
while, somewhere, a cellar starts to flood,

and the housewife banging his front-door knocker
is not surprised to find him gone,
and runs for Thwaite, who's a better worker,
and sticks at a job until it's done.

Tony Connor

42[1]

n
OthI
n
g can
s
urPas
s
the m
y
SteR
y
of
s
tilLnes
s   *E. E. Cummings*

43

may i be gay

like every lark
who lifts his life

from all the dark

who wings his why

beyond because
and sings an if

of day to yes   *E. E. Cummings*

[1]Poem numbers are those of the original edition.

44

Now i lay(with everywhere around)
me(the great dim deep sound
of rain; and of always and of nowhere)and

what a gently welcoming darkestness—

now i lay me down(in a most steep
more than music)feeling that sunlight is
(life and day are)only loaned:whereas
night is given(night and death and the rain

are given;and given is how beautifully snow)

now i lay me down to dream of(nothing
i or any somebody or you
can begin to begin to imagine)

something which nobody may keep.
now i lay me down to dream of Spring

E. E. Cummings

53

of all things under our
blonder than blondest star

the most mysterious
(eliena, my dear)is this

—how anyone so gay
possibly could die   *E. E. Cummings*

THE FOX

'Look, it's a fox!'—their two hearts spoke
Together. A fortunate day
That was when they saw him, a russet spark
Blown from the wood's long-smouldering dark
On to the woodside way.

There, on the ride, a dog fox paused.
Around him the shadows lay
Attentive suddenly, masked and poised;
And the watchers found themselves enclosed
In a circuit stronger than they.

He stood for some mystery only shared
By creatures of fire and clay.
They watched him stand with the masterless air
Of one who had the best right to be there—
Let others go or stay;

Then, with a flick of his long brush, sign
The moment and whisk it away.
Time flowed back, and the two walked on
Down the valley. They felt they were given a sign—
But of what, they could hardly say.

C. Day-Lewis

O nuclear wind, when wilt
    thou blow
  That the small rain down
    can rain?
Christ, that my love were in
    my arms
  And I had my arms again.

Paul Dehn

Ring-a-ring o' neutrons.
A pocket full of positrons,
A fission! A fission!
We all fall down.

Paul Dehn

Rain before seven,
Dead before eleven.

Paul Dehn

I had a little shadow who went in and out
with me,
And what could be the use of him was hard
for me to see
Till they took me from my Bureau looking
out across Red Square;
And when I reached Siberia, *my shadow
wasn't there.*

Paul Dehn

Rock of ages cleft for me,
Let me hide myself in thee.
While the bombers thunder past,
Shelter me from burn and blast;
And though I know all men are brothers
Let the fallout fall on others.

Paul Dehn

As with gladness men of old
Did the guiding star behold,
So with joy this starry night
They hail the latest satellite.
  Gloria in excelsis! We
    Nearer come, my God, to Thee.

Onward, Christian soldiers,
  Each to war resigned,
With the Cross of Jesus
  Vaguely kept in mind.

Paul Dehn

GUTTER PRESS

News Editor: Peer Confesses,
     Bishop Undresses,
     Torso Wrapped in Rug,
     Girl Guide Throttled,
     Baronet Bottled,
     J.P. Goes to Jug.

      But yesterday's story's
      Old and hoary.
      Never mind who got hurt.
      No use grieving,
      Let's get weaving.
      What's the latest dirt?

      Diplomat Spotted,
      Scout Garrotted,
      Thigh Discovered in Bog,
      Wrecks Off Barmouth,
      Sex In Yarmouth
      Woman In Love With Dog,
      Eminent Hostess Shoots Her Guests,
      Harrogate Lovebird Builds Two Nests.

Cameraman: *Builds two nests?*
     Shall I get a picture of the lovebird singing?
     Shall I get a picture of her pretty little eggs?
     Shall I get a picture of her babies?

News Editor: No!
      Go and get a picture of her legs.

      Beast Slays Beauty,
      Priest Flays Cutie,
      Cupboard Shows Tell-Tale Stain,
      Mate Drugs Purser,

Dean Hugs Bursar,
Mayor Binds Wife With Chain,
Elderly Monkey Marries For Money,
Jilted Junky Says 'I Want My Honey'.

Cameraman: *'Want my honey?'*
Shall I get a picture of the pollen flying?
Shall I get a picture of the golden dust?
Shall I get a picture of a queen bee?

News Editor: No!
Go and get a picture of her bust.

Judge Gets Frisky,
Nun Drinks Whisky,
Baby Found Burnt in Cot,
Show Girl Beaten,
Duke Leaves Eton—

Cameraman: *Newspaper Man Gets Shot!*
May all things clean
And fresh and green
Have mercy upon your soul,
Consider yourself paid
By the hole my bullet made—

News Editor: (*dying*) Come and get a picture of the hole.

Paul Dehn

THE WORLD I SEE

Nobody sees the world I see.
When I was small I thought the cows
And the caterpillars I kept in tins

Could see the cloud a Handley Page
Raced into another age;
I thought the ant and the bumble bee
And my brown and white pet mouse
Saw just what I saw for my sins.

'For my sins'—they so often said.
That insect, bird, fish, animal
Had no sins I knew long before
I realized they could never see
Me steal the apple from the tree.
Only the farmer could, or God.
God chalked it up against my soul,
The farmer made my bottom sore—

If he caught me—that's the point.
'What the eye doesn't . . .' you know the wink
The politician counts upon
To get your vote for a world no man
Has ever seen or ever can;
The world is always out of joint,
There's always a Hamlet to see, and think;
But the crooked kings get the business done.

The ichneumon dooms the caterpillar,
Choosing at random but never free
Not to choose; I am. And despite
The incestuous dynasties of loss
I am loth to believe man never was
Nor will be anything but a killer—
Then I look at the human world and see
The ecstatic lovers, their eyes shut tight.

Patric Dickinson

A NEW BLOCK

Three hundred fillings high
The functional sandwich soars,
All the silt of an age—
Cars shops offices dingy offices
Luxury flats flatlets
And sour on upper floors
Milk bottles marking the lonely dead.

Three thousand years down
Through how many Troys and Londons
Archaeologists probe; fragments
Of pots and forgotten tongues
Illuminate all. Why
Must we build higher Babels
The less there is to be said?

Patric Dickinson

THIS COLD UNIVERSE

These stars and planets have no names,
To name them is to lie,
I stare at this cold universe
So far from me so near to me.

How should I tame the Bear?
How steer the Plough?
I stare at this cold universe
I see into your eyes.

Above the Fell they throb and wheel
As my heart in its darkness does,
I stare at a colder universe
When I look into myself,

Marking distance, mapping void
With small 'good things of day'.
I stare at the cold universe
I reach out for your hand.

What measure is there else?
Light-years in a touch.
I stare into the darkness of myself
Where all lights may be false

Daydreams seen from a dry well—
One must have none of these
But measure the cold universe
By your mortal kiss.

Nothing must be but the sheer truth
Of love between us two:
O hand and planet eye and star
So near to me so far from me.

Patric Dickinson

JACK

My mortal husk is shelled at death
And shut inside a narrow box;
But he is coffined up in life:
Oh, what a bitter paradox!

He crouches low and supplicant,
His elbows knocking on the wood,
And with a cry too thin to hear
Implores the gods that somehow Good

Will bring him to a just release.
He waits the tapping at the locks,
He hears the children calling 'Jack!'
They think he sleeps inside his box.

They think he sleeps, but how he weeps,
His small tears falling with no sound
Like ghostly leaves that seem to fall
And fade upon a haunted ground!

We touched the lock and up he sprang,
Delight upon his simple face
As though he knew himself at last
The poet-prophet of his race—

All lowly Jacks shut up in boxes,
Composed of odds and ends of wood,
Who have such brief, amended chances
To see the world and find it good.

The children laughed and stretched their hands
And called again for Jack, for Jack,
But with a sudden brutal thrust
I caught his head and pushed him back,

Thinking, it does not do to muse
And give to toys of stick and straw
Emotions that belong to life
Lest the conclusions that we draw

Might yet be turned upon ourselves
To show each in his narrow piece
Of flesh and blood, like Jacks of straw
Shut down, and crying for release.

Rosemary Dobson

PRAYER

Lord, let me a little longer hold this peace
      Until it passes
    Like one grass among grasses;
Grant me an extension of time in this chapel of ease;
      Make idle the fear
    That my tranquillity here
Will, as too often before, brutally, suddenly cease;
      Arrange that the pain
    Will not soon come again
To beat me in pitiable anguish to my knees.

Clifford Dyment

SEA SHANTY

'I love the sea because it has drowned me,'
    Said the sailor with the coral nose.
'I love the sea because it has fed me,'
    Said the lobster with grasping claws.

'Liquid I lived and liquid I die,'
    Said the sailor with the coral nose.
'Give us this day our daily dead,'
    Said the lobster with grasping claws.

Clifford Dyment

OUTLAW

The plant grew up in the garden. Storms
    Romped through it rough as life;
Sun beat its skin to a healthy green:
    It was soon ripe for the knife,

But no one passed with an eye to take
    The plant from where it lay:
It bloomed and bore on a bed of muck
    A red child of decay.

                                        Clifford Dyment

THE DESERT

Beside a dune high as a tree
    But spreading no tree's shade
A man and boy sat silently
    Working at their trade.

A heap of bones lay on the sand
    Like barkless staves of wood;
And near it lay a second heap
    Polished with thickening blood.

One bone, two bones, three bones were
    Chosen by the man
Who made of them a heart's shape, wide
    As his two hands would span.

The man and boy sat hour by hour
    Calmly, coolly, dumb,
Feeling the scarlet heat as though
    Their blackened skins were numb.

A third heap soon rose at their side
    Like boughs laid for a pyre:
The boy's hand went to it and took
    From many lyres one lyre.

It was a lyre in shape, but where
    The stream of music springs
The lyre was nought, a mouth crying
    Wordlessly for strings.

The boy reached to the heap that shone
    Untouched on the sand
And from its bloody muteness took
    A bloody speaking hand.

He fixed the voice in place, then more,
    And soon the lyre was strung—
A frame made of three human bones,
    Each string a human tongue.

The old man took the brilliant lyre
    And struck its cords of red;
The boy rap by his side stood up
    As a snake rears up its head

And with no smile and with no sigh
    Moved to the lyre's sounds
In a world all dust save for a man,
    A dancer, and three mounds.

Clifford Dyment

MOCK EXAMINATIONS

I was invigilating an exam,
A silent room,
Pastelled perspective, tiled and confident
To curtained stage,
Old gold in the mild sunlight
Of early Spring.
And in that afternoon
The floor, the walls, the logic of the roof,
Were only aspects of the subtle light,
And all this long recession of delight,
Tile, desk and chair
Were only there
To carry humans in attentive calm,

To carry humans in attentive calm.

An hour later, on the shore,
Full tide
From the triumphant West
Where some Atlantic storm far out
Sent senseless breakers in to undermine
And strike the cliffs in regiments of line;
Great sound and water blowing air
Could not compare,
Surging grandiloquence
Was Nature's impotence;
Only that Hall, that light, had meaning
Where we planned form,
And there were children learning.

Brian Earnshaw

MEETING PEOPLE ON DOWROG

Petulant heats of summer have dried up my marsh;
Sneeze-wort, saw-wort, fleabane and dry rankness
Grow round the middle year:
The un-time
Leading to the tedium of autumn.
Wobbling on my motor-cycle,
Sad from my marsh inspection
My death of the year detection,
I saw a car draw up before me
And a plump girl leaped out to scold me.
But it was not so.
When you have taught for many years,
Britain is crossed with invisible lines
Where children, grown large, oscillate eccentrically.
Here an oscillation.
Three years ago she left,
Regretted for her vivacity,
Bright in the forbidden joys
Of going out with secondary-modern boys.

Now, briefly by the marsh:
Sneeze-wort, saw-wort and fleabane,
We could talk again,
While her latest fascinator,
Thick-lipped and amiable,
Lolled on his radiator.

Nothing to say, only old liking
Turning again in worn-out sunshine
Nothing to say, only remember
Friends carried by like leaves of November.
Briefly to re-assure her
I was the same man
Pounced through her lesson hours,

Weird, unpredictable.
There as a shadow of shadows I gestured,
Laughing and hollow at ending of summer.

Teachers to those they taught, must never age,
Nor grow in mind.
Three years we knew each other in the class,
Now by the marsh
How little truthful contact we could find.

Brian Earnshaw

STAFF LUNCH

High horse at lunchtime
With my spurs in God
Ripping at order and established worth,
Onions and spam,
I played the young freethinker
Who doesn't give a damn.

One of my pauses,
This time for sago,
One of the mistresses
Looked at me down the slanting of her eye
And blew tobacco smoke
Cynic and tired before she spoke:
'You only say what all of us
Thought a long time ago.'
'What all of us'—and none of them said no,
Pious and kind they drink their tea,
Each morning sing the unctuous hymns
That prop authority,
Each Sunday let the service go:

Sin and Redemption, masochism and woe.
Soft disillusion
Shrugs moral confusion.
Now, more than ever, I am frightened of age,
When what I think no longer angers me.

Brian Earnshaw

SENIOR DEBATING

The debate this evening
Did not go well.
I proposed Classical Music against the triviality of Pop
With easy confidence.
Carissimi and Liszt,
Some piping oboes of Bellini
Were my support, played on the gramophone.

Then I collapsed.
Arnold, from under hair and horn-rimmed glasses
Spoke against me.
Slow and deliberate, finding and meaning,
He won them from me.
I can still feel how much I failed,
Alone in the lit room
Ordering the chairs as they ran to their buses,
Measuring values.

The Head was there.
And does he feel as irrelevant as I felt,
Saddled in age,
Threadbare to sincerity?
He went out without speaking
And I shuffled chairs.
We are alone with our thoughts.
They are together in the bus with theirs.
Arnold said:

Sex is our interest
And the expression
Human to human
Of love.
In five more years
It will be over
And we will be ready for the civilized pleasure
Of jaded heart and eighteenth century measure.
Until then
Our only music is the angry beat
And stress of lovers talking
In the winter street.

The music that he played,
Furious and subtle with an impromptu that might be art,
Finished his case.
Warm with their age's solidarity
They listened and voted,
Five to thirty three.
Classical music, Arnold said, is for the imagination,
Not for reality.
So there are two states of sex.
Obsession and satiation.
All others are interludes of realization.
Obsession is elation and desire,
Active frustration and the artist's fire.
Satiation is the adult's goal
And its achievement is the end of life,
Doors closing
And films of smugness reaching round the soul.
A brief reality and then pretence,
The piping oboes
The endless compensation of the world.

Scraping the chairs behind the desks,
Glad that they had to go,
I was inclined to think that it made sense.

Brian Earnshaw

THE OLD LADIES

They had all that they wanted:
comfort, sofas well covered,
afternoon teas with crumpets,
a special, personal love.

It is possible to stop
moving, for no one will care
if you are sure that this is
what you really want. They were.

But underneath the skull's shell
an empty space grew slowly
and though they did not know it
death had happened long ago.

Marguerite Edmonds

PALLOR OF ANGELS

Wind's thin shadow
stoops across the hill
behind the silent church
where slate gravestones lurch
half lost in rough grass slopes

Carved with clasped hands
or weeping willows
each stretches back through time
The names are the same
as those still heard to-day

One grave is new
freshly piled with flowers:
a child just dead, struck down
by a backing tractor
his own father drove:
time bleeds, still raw with pain

A June sun lights
yellow walls of summer
water offered in jars
the noiseless flight of birds
Only the heart knows
the pallor of angels

Marguerite Edmonds

COLD STORAGE

Headless and hard as bricks, painted off-white,
Hanging like frozen clothes, the dead herd moves
Along the assembly line to the street
Where, in the sawdust, butchers wait with knives.

Here is no slightest hint of buttercups
And daisies, bellowing and having calves,
And Lightfoot coming to the milking shed.
Impossible also to think that shapes
Like these can grace the bodies of our loves
With soft skin and hair and glossy maidenhood.

Unlucky, then, for sacred three-in-one
We cannot correlate existences—
The rank-fat creature, the steak underdone
And oozing blood, and these clean carcasses.

Julian Ennis

APOCALYPSE

'After the New Apocalypse, very few members were still in possession of their instruments. Hardly a musician could call a decent suit his own. Yet, by the early summer of 1945, strains of sweet music floated on the air again. While the town still reeked of smoke, charred buildings and the stench of corpses, the Philharmonic Orchestra bestowed the everlasting and imperishable joy which music never fails to give.'

(from *The Muses on the Banks of the Spree*, a Berlin tourist brochure)

It soothes the savage doubts.
One Bach outweighs ten Belsens. If 200,000 people
Were remaindered at Hiroshima, the sales of So-and-So's
New novel reached a higher figure in as short a time.
So, imperishable paintings reappeared:
Texts were reprinted:
Public buildings reconstructed:
Human beings reproduced.

After the Newer Apocalypse, very few members
Were still in possession of their instruments
(Very few were still in possession of their members),
And their suits were chiefly indecent.
Yet, while the town still reeked of smoke, etc.,
The Philharmonic Trio bestowed, etc.

A civilization vindicated,
A race with three legs still to stand on!
True, the violin was shortly silenced by leukaemia,
And the pianoforte crumbled softly into dust.
But the flute was left. And one is enough.
All, in a sense, goes on. All is in order.

And the ten-tongued mammoth larks,
The forty-foot crickets and the elephantine frogs
Decided that the little chap was harmless,
At least he made no noise, on the banks of whatever river
    it used to be.

One day, a reed-warbler stepped on him by accident.
However, all, in a sense, goes on. Still the everlasting
    and imperishable joy
Which music never fails to give is being given.

D. J. Enright

VILLAGE CLASSES

Artichokes are being burnt in France,
    to keep the price up.
As Jews were once incinerated,
    to keep their price up.
(An average Jew is now worth slightly
    more than before the war.)
As O World, O Life, O Time deflower poets,
    to keep the price of poetry up.
(Not efficiently enough, though, not
    sufficiently efficiently.)
As we thin out our good intentions,
    to make them better than our bad.
As we chop down our friends,
    to keep the price of loyalty up.
As we plough back our loves,
    to enhance the value of love.
Outside the huts, vegetables are growing;
    inside, the common sorts of love.
Because, they say, the earth is like that;
    they know no modern economics.

We educate them to lay down their lives,
    to keep the price of life up.
Artichokes fetch a good price in France.
    There was always too much life in Asia.

D. J. Enright

PITCHFORK DEPARTMENT

It was patent in this ancient city, paradise of
Statuary, that pigeons ˙acked respect for greatness.
Lucky statesmen, innocent generals and forgiven thinkers,

Their iron breasts befouled, their noble brows
Turned grey, their swords and croziers rusted,
Manuscripts illuminated, paddled shanks gone leprous.

Yet the children loved the pigeons, it pleased the
Taxpayers to be used as perches. They walked our streets,
Sometimes were run over, did not despise our bread.

So the city fathers, as humane as is befitting
In this age of letters and elections, set out
Drugged fodder: 'Let the sleeping birds be stacked

With care in corporation vehicles, and conveyed to
Some remote and rural district. Let them there be laid
In appropriate positions in their proper places.'

They slept the weekend through, lost in a dream
Of the Hall of the Thirty Thousand Buddhas, or the day
When every civil servant will be issued with a public statue.

On Tuesday afternoon, from under their umbrellas,
The city fathers watched the homing pigeons, assiduous,
    unresenting,
Bowels gently stimulated, natural functions unaffected.

D. J. Enright

THE MIDDLE YEARS

Between the pale young failure
And the bloated purple success
Lie the works on the life of the dahlia
Or the shrewd financial guess.

Between the love and the yearnings
And the fat indifference of age
Lie the greatly increased earnings
And the slick best-selling page.

Between the romantic lover
And the sordid dirty old man
Lies the fruitful wasted lifetime
Of the years that also ran.

Gavin Ewart

THE DEAD

I have nothing to say to the dead
unless they approach me first.
It is their right to come to me
with a soft step, singing
or moaning as they please.

The dead cry all night under the trees.
I never tire of listening to them.
Sometimes I want to invite them in
to warm their hands by the fire
but nobody wants the dead inside,
especially not the living. Lock the door,
keep them out, they say,
or the next thing you know

they will overcome you with death,
they will feed from you, rob you,
tap your blood and your preserved memory.
The dead have no memory. A torn scarf
flows in and out of their head, controlled
by the wind of forgetfulness, not by the dead,
and where the end or the beginning may be
the dead do not know
who have no memory, no memory.

Janet Frame

COMPLAINT

The motormower a giant wasp on the lawn
reminds me that my nerves are torn.

The TV shots through the wall
do but speak of a Western Hell.

The children's quarrels and cries
tell me where my hate lies.

The traffic changing gear,
the singer without voice or ear,

the loudspeaker from the factory next door,
remind me that I've been here before

in a time quiet enough to hear a thought
parting the tangled stalks of words, creep
soft-footed from the dark into the sure trap
of light, serene light, smooth light;

the splinters piercing the once-quiet spot
remind me that thought without quiet has no shape,
that there's no escape,
that I wish either noise or I were not, were not.

Janet Frame

AUTUMN

The gate to the wood is closed said Summer.
Take the path over the pond,
kill all the daffodils.
The old men sat wrapped in greaseproof paper,
We are not afraid, they said.
Be shrewd, be whistling.
We are tired of picking locks and seasons.
All things yellow stream down beyond our eyes.

Janet Frame

SUNDAY

Sunday's thermos is filled,
Sunday's hedge clipped, car cleaned, scales played.
The plastic prayer, though it melts in the fire
is contrived in the correct shape
in a lovely contemporary colour.

Go fishing in the muddy stream
borrow an inch of beach, rent a sand fly and jellyfish
lie in bed burned bitten and stung
by the lovely contemporary wish
being granted—oh breathless—
on a flesh-coloured plastic dish.

Janet Frame

THE END OF AN AGE

The chestnut they said had stood for seventy years.
Its whiteness in May, redness in September,
Thin scrolls of long fingery twigs
   Were things expected of it.
The tree was an obvious landmark, like a hill.

The little people, hurrying about the place,
Their heads packed with intricacies,
Their feet not in the habit of standing still,
   Slightly envied the tree
For adding such tiny cubits to itself.

At last for safety's sake it had to come
And, falling, for the first time became heavy.
A man with an axe sorting it all out
   But making slow work
Said: 'A tree's complicated when it's down.'

Robin Fulton

A NOTE FOR ROBERT HENRYSON

winter can't have changed much for us,
the shape of windows perhaps but not the hard
flowers on them the weak sun can't soften

four walls have a lot to keep out
still and much the same to keep in,
a fire a book whisky and common sense

from me to you is not many miles,
we could walk together now and on the snow
our hunchback shadows would be like twins

your outer weather then I understand
and almost your inner: late medieval
though to you not yet so far past
and still rich with clarity and fear

Robin Fulton

THE SNAKE

at dawn this morning the air was thick and white
the winter people nodded 'It won't last'
holes in fences were half full, clean
windows were smudged again with spittle sleet
on your face at one touch it was water
on streets it was pale mud, on garden beds
it was imperceptibly sucked in

in the spring snow I thought of a grey house
squareset in a square garden, watched
over by a war-memorial clock
whose bells box in each hour
with four quarters—spring must be late
there, buds on apple trees hard
soft cuttings on indoor racks

on a shelf in the porch in a haircream jar
an adder in formalin, multiple S
(if you opened it now would the bends pull straight?)
black and yellow are near-grey and near-grey
if you shake it specks of decomposition
whirl in a miniature toy snowstorm
the eyes though still stare you out

safe in spirit safe in the sealed jar
deaf to the bells
it is long since the frightened gardener
thrashed it— I doubt if he thought of Christ's heel
or Achilles'
          the snow steams and shrivels by noon
the gardener is still there years on
padding in rich dirt his gems of seed

Robin Fulton

RACE

When I returned to my home town
believing that no one would care
who I was and what I thought
it was as if the people caught
an echo of me everywhere
they knew my story by my face
and I who am always alone
became a symbol of my race

Like every living Jew I have
in imagination seen
the gas-chamber the mass-grave
the unknown body which was mine
and found in every German face
behind the mask the mark of Cain
I will not make their thoughts my own
by hating people for their race

Karen Gershon

IN A TRAM

I felt most alone when I was surrounded by Germans
who would have sent me to Riga twenty-five years ago
I knew of no means by which I might have determined
their real present reaction to meeting a Jew

What distinguishes these who tolerated the slaughter
from people elsewhere whom they seem to resemble so much
did they recognize in me a murdered couple's daughter
does their instinct no longer respond to a Jew within reach

People in trams have decided their destination
they would not have broken the threads of their lives for a
   Jew
had they turned upon me I would have felt less forsaken
I meant nothing to them and they mattered so much to me

Karen Gershon

THE CROWS

Crows will stick their beaks into anything.
Ugliness protects them: children don't care
to pet them, and when they descend on trees,
eagles discreetly go somewhere quieter.

They will sit on balconies and appear
to comment on passing traffic. Their black
cloak never conceals the dagger of speech,
their communal weapon. They talk, talk, talk.

I've heard them break the silence of night
with sudden loud cawing as if provoked
into dispute by a falling star,
and then flying skywards as though to look

up some evidence, keen as scientists;
yet really, when you see their missions
come mostly to nothing, they appear more
like intensely dedicated politicians.

Zulfikar Ghose

THE MISSION

For sixty years or more the mission church
has let the lantern of its chalk-white walls
so shine before the shouting mountain men
that some slight shift of soul may well
be posited.

The sabbath drums boom out their routine summons
among the candled coral trees—and down
the mountain's grassy runnels tribesmen pour
to worship and the whitewashed walls resound
with battered diatonic hymns.

The preacher preaches love: love one another.
(How can we love the plainsmen when they burn
our houses, steal our goats and rape our wives?
We'll love all men as Master Jesus did
except the lowlanders.)

On Monday noon the curling fleece of smoke
dilates above the plainsmen's huts. And down
crash axed banana trees. And leg-trussed goats
stagger and scream. Above the bedlam hangs
the white star of persistent Christ.

David Gill

THE TWO WITCHES

O sixteen hundred and ninety one,
Never was year so well begun,
Backsy-forsy and inside out,
The best of all years to ballad about.

On the first fine day of January
I ran to my sweetheart Margery
And tossed her over the roof so far
That down she fell like a shooting star.

But when we two had frolicked and kissed
She clapped her fingers about my wrist
And tossed me over the chimney stack,
And danced on me till my bones did crack.

Then, when she had laboured to ease my pain,
We sat by the stile of Robin's Lane,
She in a hare and I in a toad
And puffed at the clouds till merry they glowed.

We spelled our loves until close of day.
I wished her good-night and walked away,
But she put out a tongue that was long and red
And swallowed me down like a crumb of bread.

Robert Graves

THE HUNG WU VASE

With women like Marie no holds are barred.
Where do they get the gall? How can they do it?

She stormed out, slamming the hall door so hard
That a vase on the gilt shelf above—you knew it,
Loot from the Summer Palace at Pekin
And worth the entire contents of my flat—
Toppled and fell . . .
                          I poured myself straight gin,
Downing it at a gulp. 'So that was that!'

The bell once more . . . Marie walked calmly in,
Observed broken red porcelain on the mat,
Looked up, looked down again with condescension,
Then, gliding past me to retrieve a glove
(Her poor excuse for this improper call),
Muttered: 'And one thing I forgot to mention:
Your Hung Wu vase was phoney, like your love!'

How can they do it? Where do they get the gall?

Robert Graves

IANTO THE UNDERTAKER

Ianto undertakes by trade, though only assistant
these long years to John Mawr. Short and swarthy,
Iberian Ianto embalms the dead, loves his trade.
'It's bloody good mun,' he said to me,
in undertones so that John wouldn't hear,
'it's a good living, this looking after the dead.'
He told me of the way the corpses contract,
creak and coil after death; of the way
that cries break from bodies now without breath.
'Don't tell John Mawr,' he said furtively,
'but there's some good pickings, too, you see,
for the families often leave gold rings
on the fingers of the dead—

but I get them before they go down the hole!'
'But how do you manage to remove the rings,'
I questioned, 'with the fingers so stiff and swollen?'
'Simple boy,' he said with pride, 'they *are* stiff,
I admit, but I just break the bloody fingers
clean off, see—snap them like carrots I do!
Would you like to see my collection of wedding rings?'
I declined, and he continued, eager to tell,
'the job's got a good future, you know,
there's no slumps in this trade; constant it is.'
He turned back to work on his treasured coffins then,
and I walked on down Llangarw's narrow main street—
seeing for a moment his black-nailed hands
scurrying like furred spiders
over the slow rictus of the fading dead flesh.

Bryn Griffiths

A NOTE FOR R. S. THOMAS

Come down, Mr Thomas, from the pain
Of your austere perch, the imposed rigour of thought,
Your stern pulpit of cymric rock.
Take back your bleak sermons on us—
The stone desert in the peasant's mind,
The slow decay of an old race,
The stone hearts in the mountain flowers.

We, the same old stock, know a different story—
Yes, you have caught *one* facet of truth,
But, as you should know, there are many others.
There are colours burning still in the peasant's brain;
The old language still lives in the quick tongues . . .
They, the English and others, fell for the tale—
But we, part of you, know it too well.

Two thousand years of assault and conquest
Have failed to kill this race rooted in rock,
Failed to extinguish the slow flame of speech.
We have always been in retreat—but then,
Viewing the past, cannot we continue as a nation,
As a brilliant island in this day's uniform sea?

The bible of your mind reads like a parched desert—
No oasis burns in the blind memory of you!
Beside the granite uplands, the stone plateaus of despair,
There remain the green valleys,
The bright chambers of changeless air.

Bryn Griffiths

AUTUMN DAY · RAINER MARIA RILKE

Lord: it is Time. The summer was so good.
Now lay your shadows on the sundial's face
And let the winds run loose on field and wood.

Let the last fruits grow full upon the vine;
Give to them still two southern summer days,
Force them to their perfection now and chase
The last sweetness into the heavy wine.

Who has no house, by now, will build no more,
Who's now alone, will long remain ungiven,
Will watch, and read, and, his long letters written,
Will on the garden paths back and forth
Restlessly wander when the leaves are driven.

Charles Gullans

THE SOVEREIGN HOTEL, SANTA MONICA

In lobby, lounge, or restaurant they sink
Deep in their chairs, regard the empty wall,
And stroke their pearls, their foxes, and their mink,
As the indolence of age assaults them all.

Cosmetically preserved by tint and glaze,
Vague intimations of another time,
Of youth and beauty, animate their gaze,
Quicken their features in outrageous mime.

Empty almost of pride and vanity,
They have outlived their husbands and their friends:
Embalmed in pensions, bonds, annuities,
They aimlessly await their separate ends.

Old reptiles lounging in the southern sun,
They are not tender and they are not meek;
Their eyes acknowledge that their age has won
An ease so precious that they scarcely speak.

Ancient with terrors that they cannot gauge,
They will not slacken vulgarly to death.
Motion and motive stilled, their love, their rage,
Is quiet, and they live now breath by breath.

Charles Gullans

BY THE NORTH SEA

A Roman road took us from the village of Bradwell-
 on-Sea through marshy crop farms down to the shore
 on a ridge which was so gradual

my friend had to point it out. Yet in a tidal flood
 the road is a strip of dry land in a plain
 of water. Now the sloping meadows

erupted with the lean daffodils of March. We walked
 tilting our bodies against the Northern wind.
 In the ditches there were crumbling rows

of four-foot concrete trylons. 'One Sunday in nineteen-
 forty, we set branches in the largest fields
 to stop the gliders.' A radar screen

turned in its arc to the north, looking out to the sea,
 and gulls swooped at the Nuclear Power Station
 as if it were a ship. Beyond it

the estuary washed inland as far as Maldon,
 and tied near the banks were the left-over bodies
 of freighters and tankers hung on chains,

the trash of a long war, and of an economy
 of sailors. Ahead of us, where the road struck
 straight at the sea, the afternoon sun

illuminated a narrow stone barn. 'St Peter's,'
 said my friend, 'where Bishop Cedd made his mission
 to Saxons in six-hundred-fifty.'

It backed up close to the cold sea that expected it,
 like the last king of a defeated nation
 beaten from its plains by invaders.

The sun made black shadows within the stone and tile wall,
   as rough as if the sea wind had worked at it
      to raise the surfaces like landscape.

'The new brick of the side is where farmers hacked a door
   to turn it into a barn. It was only
      eighty-odd years ago that someone

'saw that it was Cedd's St Peter's, and changed it again
   back to a church.' The Bishop had scavenged tiles
      from the Roman fort of Othona

which had held the mouth of the estuary against
   Saxon pillagers, until the Romans left
      to defend their own city. Inside,

rubble was heaped in the corners. It was a bare room
   without grace or comfort. More bricks had filled in
      Cedd's narrow arches, but the colour

of the new brick revealed the old shapes. We went outside
   and found a piece of the thick wall which remains
      of Othona. 'Out there in the marsh,'

my friend told me, 'when they made tank trenches they dug up
   cartloads of Roman sea-wall. We were waiting
      for a new invasion from the sea.'

We walked for a moment under the noise of the gulls,
   and then returned to the village, on the road
      which keeps its head out of water.

Donald Hall

THE POEM

It discovers by night
what the day hid from it.
Sometimes it turns itself
into an animal.
In summer it takes long walks
by itself where meadows
fold back from ditches.
Once it stood still
in a quiet row of machines.
Who knows
what it is thinking?

Donald Hall

OMENS

1

The year opens with frozen pipes,
Roads impassable, cars immovable,
Letter delivery slow;
But smallpox from Pakistan
Carried fast from Yorkshire to Surrey,
And no lack of news:
In the Andes a landslide
That buried a town;
In Dalmatia, earthquakes;
Bush fires around Melbourne,
Cooking wallabies, koala bears.
In the Congo, another rebellion;
In Algeria, random murders on either side;
Paris a playground for thugs.

2

The milk our children drink may or may not be poisoned
By last year's fall-out, no longer part of the news.

Our earth may be shrinking, expanding
But was found to contain great cracks
That will doubtless widen even without our help.

3

Amid such omens
How do we dare to live?
Brashly building, begetting
For a town besieged,
Crumbling, patched again, crumbling
And undermined?

4

Deeper I gulp cold air that not too suddenly kills,
Greedily drink with my eyes the winter sunshine and clouds,
The old white horse in the meadow
Green again after snow.

Next year I shall see no meadow, no horse.

Michael Hamburger

SECURITY

1

So he's got there at last, been received as a partner—
In a firm going bankrupt;
Found the right place (walled garden), arranged for
    a mortgage—
But they're pulling the house down
To make room for traffic.

Worse winds are rising. He takes out new policies
For his furniture, for his life,
At a higher premium
Against more limited risks.

Who can face the winds, till the panes crack in their frames?
And if a man faced them, what in the end could he do
But look for shelter like all the rest?
The winds too are afraid, and blow from fear.

3

I hear my children at play
And recall that one branch of the elm-tree looks dead;
Also that twenty years ago now I could have been parchment
Cured and stretched for a lampshade,
Who now have children, a lampshade
And the fear of those winds.

I saw off the elm-tree branch
To find that the wood was sound;
Mend the fences yet again,
Knowing they'll keep out no one,
Let alone the winds.
For still my children play,
And shall tomorrow, if the weather holds.

Michael Hamburger

TERRA INCOGNITA

*'During the flight I saw for the first time with my
own eyes the earth's spherical shape'—
Major Gagarin: 13th April 1961*

See her then swing through space, another moon
    Wrapped in a shining singleness, an Earth
That no division knows nor count of time,
    Nor name for war and peace, dying and birth:

See her with mountains, but no barriers,
    Countries, but countries by no owner claimed,
Continents linked in passionless embrace
    Neither by greeds nor loyalties inflamed.

If such the bright impersonal wanderer—
    No guarded frontiers, no jealous dates—
Such too the unknown Earth on which we walk,
    Hid by our map of human loves and hates.

George Rostrevor Hamilton

TURKEYS OBSERVED

One observes them, one expects them;
Blue-breasted in their indifferent mortuary,
Beached bare on the cold marble slabs
In immodest underwear frills of feather.

The red sides of beef retain
Some of the smelly majesty of living:
A half-cow slung from a hook maintains
That blood and flesh are not ignored.

But a turkey cowers in death.
Pull his neck, pluck him, and look—
He is just another poor forked thing,
A skin bag plumped with inky putty.

He once complained extravagantly
In an overture of gobbles;
He lorded it on the claw-flecked mud
With a grey flick of his Confucian eye.

Now, as I pass the bleak Christmas dazzle,
I find him ranged with his cold squadrons:
The fuselage is bare, the proud wings snapped,
The tail-fan stripped down to a shameful rudder.

Seamus Heaney

DOCKER

There, in the corner, staring at his drink.
The cap juts like a gantry's crossbeam,
Cowling plated forehead and sledgehead jaw.
Speech is clamped in the lips' vice.

That fist would drop a hammer on a Catholic—
Oh yes, that kind of thing could start again;
The only Roman collar he tolerates
Smiles all round his sleek pint of porter.

Mosaic imperatives bang home like rivets;
God is a foreman with certain definite views
Who orders life in shifts of work and leisure.
A factory horn will blare the Resurrection.

He sits, strong and blunt as a Celtic cross,
Clearly used to silence and an armchair:
Tonight the wife and children will be quiet
At slammed door and smoker's cough in the hall.

Seamus Heaney

THE PLAY WAY

Sunlight pillars through glass; probes each desk
For milk-tops, sour drinking straws, old crusts.
The music strides to challenge it
Mixing memory and desire with chalk dust.

My lesson note reads: Teacher will play
Beethoven's Concerto Number Five
And class will express themselves freely
In writing. One said 'Can we jive?'

When I produced the record but now
The big sound has silenced them. Higher
And firmer each authoritative note
Pumps the classroom up tight as a tyre,

Working its private spell behind eyes
That stare wide: they have forgotten me
For once. Pencils are chewed, tongues mime
Their blundering embrace of the free

Word. A silence charged with sweetness
Breaks short on lost faces where I see
New looks. Then notes stretch taut as snares. They trip
To fall into themselves unknowingly.

Seamus Heaney

THE BED BUG

The bed bug is like Cain
A wanderer on the face of the earth—
Perpetual immigrant,
Being an intimate lover of Man;
An exiguous Count Dracula.

By nature he is sub-tropical:
He likes warm places—snug
As a bug in a rug.

His name, I fancy, is originally Arabic
(He returned with us from the Crusades)
But 'contaminated', as philologists say,
With anglo-Saxon *bug*—'goblin' or 'devil'
(Cf. Slavonic *Bog* = 'God').

I have been eaten by bed bugs
In three continents so far:
Those in the Parisian Latin Quarter
Were certainly the worst
(They had had Villon and Verlaine before).

A ruthless spraying of DDT,
Burning sulphur, arsenical smoke-bombs
Will get rid of bed bugs. But the natives
Generally seem to prefer to be bitten
Until they become immune from the irritation.

Or you can simply learn to sleep with the light on:
The bug is afraid of light.
But this is to take a rather Manichaean attitude—
Exchange of blood with any of God's creatures

Is (as of course John Donne knew)
A matter with serious implications.
It has something to do with love.

America has a variety
Known as the 'kissing bug' . . .

John Heath-Stubbs

THE STARLING

The starling is my darling, although
I don't much approve of its
Habits. Proletarian bird,
Nesting in holes and corners, making a mess,
And sometimes dropping its eggs
Just any old where—on the front lawn, for instance.

It thinks it can sing too. In springtime
They are on every rooftop, or high bough,
Or telegraph pole, blithering away
Discords, with clichés picked up
From the other melodists.

But go to Trafalgar Square,
And stand, about sundown, on the steps of St Martin's;
Mark then in the air,
The starlings, before they roost, at their evolutions—
Scores of starlings, wheeling,
Streaming and twisting, the whole murmuration
Turning like one bird: an image
Realized, of the City.

John Heath-Stubbs

THE TORTOISE

Always to be at home
For the tortoise may be as burdensome
As for the human being,
His continuing exile:

The foxes have hide-outs,
The birds of the air their cradles—
They are free to come and go:
To the tortoise, his dome.

'Stroking, a waste of time,'
(Said Sydney Smith) 'You might as well think,
Caressing St Paul's, to please
The dean and Chapter.'

But was wrong,
For he is sensitive,
Even to the roof-tops;
Vegetarian, inoffensive, longaeval,
Condemned, through seven generations
Of men, to trundle
The load of his home-keeping.

John Heath-Stubbs

POETRY TODAY

The sun is eclipsed; and one by one
The birds stop singing—
Folded their wings:

But I never heard
That the frogs stopped croaking.

John Heath-Stubbs

'IT OUT-HERODS HEROD. PRAY YOU, AVOID IT.'

Tonight my children hunch
Toward their Western, and are glad
As, with a Sunday punch,
The Good casts out the Bad.

And in their fairy tales
The warty giant and witch
Get sealed in doorless jails
And the match-girl strikes it rich.

I've made myself a drink.
The giant and witch are set
To bust out of the clink
When my children have gone to bed.

All frequencies are loud
With signals of despair;
In flash and morse they crowd
The rondure of the air.

For the wicked have grown strong,
Their numbers mock at death,
Their cow brings forth its young,
Their bull engendereth.

Their very fund of strength,
Satan, bestrides the globe;
He stalks its breadth and length
And finds out even Job.

Yet by quite other laws
My children make their case;
Half God, half Santa Claus,
But with my voice and face,

A hero comes to save
The poorman, beggarman, thief,
And make the world behave
And put an end to grief.

And that their sleep be sound
I say this childermas
Who could not, at one time,
Have saved them from the gas.

Antony Hecht

ADMARSH CHURCH
BLEASDALE

The voice of God strikes coldly in this place—
Cold stone, grey light, black Bible on the back
Of a brass-winged eagle, and an unseen face
That binds the hesitant soul in bands of black.

But first—the lych-gate leading from the moor
To a tidy graveyard walled against the wild
Wind-trampled woods and heather, where the poor
May sleep the long sleep, being reconciled
To the tyrant soil that claims them in the end.

What shall we pray for, shut in from the sun—
For peace on earth
Or war among the creatures? For the one
United Good to close the rifts of birth?
Or shall we turn and run
Back to the fells and asking not, accept
The fundamental conflict, and be glad
For what is there?
We speak a wordless universal prayer
Expecting no reply.
Only the fields and the undemanding sky
Open their book to us and they are dumb.

The church door slams before a lawless wind;
The lonely clock strikes four;
Cold shadow-pillars thicken on the floor
As we turn and leave the vaulted dark behind.

Out on the open moor, release is good;
The wind flows round us and the thinning wood
Rains leaves about our ears.
The question clears; we follow the rough road on
Where others follow and the rest have gone.

Phoebe Hesketh

THE FOX

It was twenty years ago I saw the fox
Gliding along the edge of prickling corn,
A nefarious shadow
Between the emerald field and bristling hedge,
On velvet feet he went.

The wind was kind, withheld from him my scent
Till my threaded gaze unmasked him standing there,
The colour of last year's beech-leaves, pointed black,
Poised, uncertain, quivering nose aware
Of danger throbbing through each licking leaf.
One foot uplifted, balanced on the brink
Of perennial fear, the hunter hunted stood.

I heard no alien stir in the friendly wood,
But the fox's sculpted attitude was tense
With scenting, listening, with a seventh sense
Flaring to the alert; I heard no sound
Threaten the morning; and followed his amber stare,
But in that hair-breadth moment, that flick of the eye,
He vanished.

And now, whenever I hear the expectant cry
Of hounds on the empty air,
I look to a gap in the hedge and see him there
Filling the space with fear; the trembling leaves
Are frozen in his stillness till I hear
His leashed-up breathing—how the stretch of time
Contracts within the flash of re-creation!

Phoebe Hesketh

THE FROG PRINCE

He was cold as slime,
Coloured to the underside
Of a rotted leaf
Mottled brown and yellow.

With promises of princehood underneath
The skin—if warmed by love—
He chose my pillow
For his transformation,
Croaked at me to stroke his throat
Pulsing like a swamp-bubble.

Pity froze to contempt;
Rather than touch him I lifted the pillow,
Flung him into the night.

Now alone in autumn mood I wonder
Who is this tall young man
Supple as willow and wind,
Carrying the sun on his shoulder.
His light shafts through me to its mark
In a girl not beautiful, but kind.

Phoebe Hesketh

THE DARK SIDE OF THE MOON

Twenty hundred and twenty-five:
Freedom from need to stay alive.
This man-machine can think and act
More clearly; matter sticks to fact
And metal makes no claims; each part
Works perfectly without a heart.

No woman made grotesque with child—
The Super-Incubator smiled
On trays of re-conditioned eggs:
'We're going to breed 'em without legs—
They've moved around so long on wheels.
Our product neither sees nor feels
And wastes no time, and if it tires
We raise the voltage, change the wires.
No need for clothing, beds, or food
In dehydrated man, no crude
Relationships to reproduce
Obedient creatures for our use.
Metal and brain have long combined
Over the old illusion, Mind,
For we have found the reason Why
Behind the curtain of the sky.

The dark side of the moon is ours
Forbidden to men and beasts and flowers—
A foolproof Eden in the plan
To substitute our image for man.
We, the machine-gods without breath,
Have conquered time and space and death!'

Phoebe Hesketh

PROVINCIAL UNDERGRADUATE

The draggled hair, stained sweater, rumpled slacks,
Eyes staring angrily out of a young face,
Hand nervously dabbing a cigarette
Out against a wall as though it was somebody's face.
He grunts, not argues, grins rather than laughs when
Somebody's tried to do something and failed again.

That somebody! How he hates him! Whoever he is—
From a better school, maybe, or dressed up to kill,
Who can grow a beard, throw parties, pay out cash,
Who can always get the prettiest girls at will.
He covertly kicks his ankles in a queue,
Or lounges across his path. What else can he do?

'After puberty, only the glands want to learn'
Says Goole who weighs up students at a sneer
And finds them wanting. Wanting to get out and earn,
Wanting to be loved, respected,—maybe, feared.
A place in the world? A good job? Goole, you
Failed to teach him what else there was to do.

What else *is* there? He's got to get a degree
Somehow, writes essays on half-known facts.
They're ticked, gone over, somehow rejected. He
Must do better next time, re-read, re-think, go back—
Go back in anger, resign, though not resigned,
Looking for what he does not want to find.

Philip Hobsbaum

LOGRIA

None wept to see the garrisons depart,
for corn stood high beneath the generous sun;
that year the farmers prospered, beasts were fat,
though markets dwindled in the emptying towns.
Grass thrust between the crumbling paving stones,
no wreath hung on the tall triumphal arch;
none mourned that the tax-gatherers had gone,
or longed to hear the legionaries' march.
That year the cup of plenty seemed to be
held overflowing at bright summer's lips;
none heard, across the grey unfriendly sea,
the knock of hammers building dragon ships.

David Holliday

POMPEII

Markets, temples, warehouses and wide
paved streets, tree-shaded squares where stood
bombastic statues of dead magnates, showed
a laudable and decent civic pride;
while on the sloping, fertile mountain side,
farmsteads and vineyards studded on the rich
dark soil displayed those self-same virtues which
had made the city wealthy, dignified
with public buildings, opulent white
marble terraces and glittering domes;
the brothels, barracks, and the sprawling slums
kept decently secluded, out of sight.
A thriving city, careful, prosperous:
but in the mountain's throat red lava rose.

David Holliday

THE SONG OF THE SPECTATORS

We are the lookers-on; we can spectate
Street holes and accidents with equal love.
We have one rule: 'Do not participate
But scan events always from one remove.'

I'm told we stood six hours while darkness grew,
To hear a nailed man with pity cry:
'Forgive them for they know not what they do.'
Next day, we came to watch another die.

As women, we counted dropped stitches and heads;
One plain, one aristo, one purl, one child.
Then we went home to good plebeian beds
Our working and class conscience reconciled.

The day they burnt Joan in the market square
We came early to watch them build the pyre;
And when she screamed for mercy from us there
One of us threw a stick to feed the fire.

We watched on railway platforms as they piled
Waggon after waggon full of Jews one day,
And did not ask 'Where to?' but only smiled
And said 'There go the Jews', and turned away.

Years later, in a glass-walled cage, a man
Said he'd obeyed the orders he'd been sent;
And we knew he was nothing other than
A Watcher, like us, trapped in an Event.

We know that we, the onlookers, create
The spectacle, and too, we recognize
That we survive by being separate.
It is only the participant who dies.

But one day, with blank eyes, we will watch a bomb fall
That will eat its creators—good citizens all.

Mary Horton

THE EAVESDROPPERS
(Old French ballad, *circa* 1942)

'Mother, what is that sound I hear?'
'Only the sea, sighing.'
'No, this sound is nerve-end near.'
'The war-planes are flying.'

'Mother, I hear the sound again.'
    'Only the wind calling.'
'It is a sound of living pain.'
    'The black bombs are falling.'

'Mother, this is a cry of fear.'
    'Only a dog, howling.'
'No, it's not a *dog* I hear.'
    'The great guns are growling.'

'Mother, I can hear it still.'
    'Only the gulls screaming.'
'It comes from the camp on the hill.'
    'Child, you have been dreaming.'

'Mother, that sound is centuries clear,
    And only *you* are lying.
Why don't you tell me that I hear
    The Jews, dying?'

(During the war, I lived near a German forced-labour camp. When the wind was in the right direction, we could sometimes hear people crying.)

Mary Horton

AWAKENING

I was not wearier where I lay
All night on the iron floor
Than many nights, nor felt the rope
Eat at my wrists and ankles more;

And when they brought the engine in
And tried the wheels, let the jaws meet,
Muttered, and set the pincers ready
And blew the fire to the right heat,

I did not fear or feel. The mind
Was dried and shrunk away. Their eyes
Looked only on dumb degraded flesh,
Sunk beyond horror or surprise.

Until a maid came in with tankards
For these good fellows; and at the door
Turned with one glance of pity to
The thing I was upon the floor.

It was this drop of succour woke
Staring terror, screaming pain
In every nerve and cell. Her look
Called up a living man again.

Graham Hough

DEATH IN THE VILLAGE

All afternoon she held her vague dark eyes
Bent to the window where an apple tree
Dandled its fruit and leant against the pane;
And it was through a drift of tangled leaves
That the two children she had never had
Ran home from school and whispered in the lane.

At four o'clock the husband she had not loved
Trudged round the corner, lifted up the latch
And through the slanting door let in the gold;
Turning her head she felt the chill strong breath,
And even as she waited for the kiss
Saw on his sleeve the grey churchyard mould.

And then the kettle sang, and as she stepped
Towards the kitchen threshold, there were two

Who many a year ago had courted her;
And she had not been kind; but there they were
Come back again, one brown with blazing eyes,
The other pale with seaweed in his hair.

A dear disorder stirred the ordered place
As all at once their voices filled the room
And dipped and circled in the air above her,
And chimed and sang and beat the silence back
In one accord, past all contention now,
Treble and bass, husband and child and lover.

She had no time to ask why they had come,
For all the voices seemed to speak one thought.
'We waited long,' they said. 'Now you are free
To come with us.' And as they crowded round,
Smiling and calm, they held her and were gone,
Before she even thought to make the tea.

The kettle hissed alone and soon burned dry;
The clock struck five; the fire died. It was years
Since kin or company had crossed the floor.
Only the cat picked out with mincing feet
His delicate way among the carpet flowers;
And all the rippled quiet lay smooth once more.

Graham Hough

THISTLES

Against the rubber tongues of cows and the hoeing hands
    of men
Thistles spike the summer air
And crackle open under a blue-black pressure.

Every one a revengeful burst
Of resurrection, a grasped fistful
Of splintered weapons and Icelandic frost thrust up

From the underground stain of a decayed Viking.
They are like pale hair and the gutturals of dialects.
Every one manages a plume of blood.

Then they grow grey like men.
Mown down, it is a feud. Their sons appear
Stiff with weapons, fighting back over the same ground.

Ted Hughes

PIKE

Pike, three inches long, perfect
Pike in all parts, green tigering the gold.
Killers from the egg: the malevolent aged grin.
They dance on the surface among the flies.

Or move, stunned by their own grandeur,
Over a bed of emerald, silhouette
Of submarine delicacy and horror.
A hundred feet long in their world.

In ponds, under the heat-struck lily pads—
Gloom of their stillness:
Logged on last year's black leaves, watching upwards,
Or hung in an amber cavern of weeds

The jaws' hooked clamp and fangs
Not to be changed at this date;
A life subdued to its instrument;
The gills kneading quietly, and the pectorals.

Three we kept behind glass,
Jungled in weed: three inches, four,
And four and a half: fed fry to them—
Suddenly there were two. Finally one

With a sag belly and the grin it was born with.
And indeed they spare nobody.
Two, six pounds each, over two feet long,
High and dry and dead in the willow-herb—

One jammed past its gills down the other's gullet:
The outside eye stared: as a vice locks—
The same iron in this eye
Though its film shrank in death.

A pond I fished, fifty yards across,
Whose lilies and muscular tench
Had outlasted every visible stone
Of the monastery that planted them—

Stilled legendary depth:
It was as deep as England. It held
Pike too immense to stir, so immense and old
That past nightfall I dared not cast

But silently cast and fished
With the hair frozen on my head
For what might move, for what eye might move.
The still splashes on the dark pond,

Owls hushing the floating woods
Frail on my ear against the dream
Darkness beneath night's darkness had freed,
That rose slowly towards me, watching.

Ted Hughes

BULLFROG

With their lithe long strong legs
Some frogs are able
To thump upon double-
Bass strings though pond-water deadens and clogs.

But you, bullfrog, you pump out
Whole fogs full of horn—a threat
As of a liner looming. True
That, first hearing you
Disgorging your gouts of darkness like a wounded god,
Not utterly fantastical I expected
(As in some antique tale depicted)
A broken-down bull up to its belly in mud,
Sucking black swamp up, belching out black cloud

And a squall of gudgeon and lilies.
                                        A surprise,
To see you, a boy's prize,
No bigger than a rat—all dumb silence
In your little old woman hands.

Ted Hughes

THE RETIRED COLONEL

Who lived at the top end of our street
Was a Mafeking stereotype, ageing.
Came, face pulped scarlet with kept rage,
For air past our gate.
Barked at his dog knout and whipcrack
And cowerings of India: five or six wars
Stiffened in his reddened neck;
Brow bull-down for the stroke.

Wife dead, daughters gone, lived on
Honouring his own caricature.
Shot through the heart with whisky wore
The lurch like ancient courage, would not go down
While posterity's trash stood, held
His habits like a last stand, even
As if he had Victoria rolled
In a Union Jack in that stronghold.

And what if his sort should vanish?
The rabble starlings roar upon
Trafalgar. The man-eating British lion
By a pimply age brought down.
Here's his head mounted, though only in rhymes,
Beside the head of the last English
Wolf (those starved gloomy times!)
And the last sturgeon of Thames.

Ted Hughes

HAWK ROOSTING

I sit in the top of the wood, my eyes closed.
Inaction, no falsifying dream
Between my hooked head and hooked feet:
Or in sleep rehearse perfect kills and eat.

The convenience of the high trees!
The air's buoyancy and the sun's ray
Are of advantage to me;
And the earth's face upward for my inspection.

My feet are locked upon the rough bark.
It took the whole of Creation
To produce my foot, my each feather:
Now I hold Creation in my foot

Or fly up, and revolve it all slowly—
I kill where I please because it is all mine.
There is no sophistry in my body:
My manners are tearing off heads—

The allotment of death.
For the one path of my flight is direct
Through the bones of the living.
No arguments assert my right:

The sun is behind me.
Nothing has changed since I began.
My eye has permitted no change.
I am going to keep things like this.

                                        Ted Hughes

PENNINES IN APRIL

If this country were a sea (that is solid rock
Deeper than any sea) these hills heaving
Out of the east, mass behind mass, at this height
Hoisting heather and stones to the sky
Must burst upwards and topple into Lancashire.

Perhaps, as the earth turns, such ground-stresses
Do come rolling westward through the locked land.
Now, measuring the miles of silence
Your eye takes the strain: through

Landscapes gliding blue as water
Those barrellings of strength are heaving slowly and heave
To your feet and surf upwards
In a still, fiery air, hauling the imagination,
Carrying the larks upward.

                                        Ted Hughes

CHURCH SCHOOL

The graves pressed to the windows. At
   My elbow I could see
The tombstones of old parish clerks
   Stood staring in on me;

Gaunt leaning shapes of churchwardens,
   And sextons, row by row;
And back of them the village dead
   A-crowding on tiptoe.

I gave them little heed. Was none
   Disturbed my thinking save
For that which fronted me all day—
   A small forsaken grave

That clutched a rosy spindle tree,
   And else was laid alone;
Railed in till none could pluck a weed
   Or cleanse the bitten stone;

The sleeping place, a hundred years,
   Of one Joanna Wilde;
'Eight summers . . .' spoke the crumbling lines,
   'Good scholar, gentle child . . .'

No more. The mosses ate the rest.
   But times when all was still
I thought upon Joanna Wilde,
   And pondered her until

She all but stood before me in
   Her sober woollen dress,
Her pinafore drawn straight and starched
   About her littleness;

Until I knew her braided hair,
　　The solemn-lidded look
Turned on her ciphering; the way
　　She held her spelling book;

Until it seemed that I could touch
　　The diligent small hands
That stitched unending calicoes
　　And timeless linen bands;

And that a word of praise would bring
　　A colour to her cheek,
And she would smile, a brief shy smile,
　　And lift her head and speak,

And tell me if she heard the bell,
　　And if she grieved to be
So long away from school. . . . But here
　　My sense took hold of me

And I would thrust off foolishness,
　　And rise and dim the light,
And leave the desks and tombstones to
　　The darkness and the night.

One afternoon the mist came down;
　　We scarce could see the wall;
The windows blacked; there was no sky
　　Nor any graves at all.

I drew my children to the fire,
　　And warm they sat and gay;
But—oh—it seemed a bitter thing
　　To lie outside that day;

And all at once I heard my heart
　　Run crying sharp and thin,

As like as not her mother called,
    'Joanna, child, come in!'

Should the door have swung? The door
    Stayed on its latch, and fast;
No soft wet footprints tracked the floor;
    No shivering air slid past.

No sounds were there but living sounds;
    The crack of burning wood;
And presently my level voice
    Telling them Red Riding Hood.

But—two full days the darkness held;
    Two mornings by my chair
We found bright spindle sprays, and none
    Could tell who laid them there.

The third day—and the light came back;
    The graves showed washed and green;
The robins sang, and all things were
    As ever they had been;

Except the broken spindle tree,
    Its branches bare and blind;
And something sitting quiet in
    A corner of my mind.

I do not shun Joanna's grave.
    I have no fear of her.
But when the morning comes with mist
    I take the register

And call the fifty names with haste,
    And mark them and have done;
Nor count the heads, lest once again
    There should be fifty-one.   *Ada Jackson*

OUR BROTHER RICHARD

He went his own rake-helly way;
He gamed and diced and swore.
Bred up in fear and godliness,
He loved the tavern more.

Our father drove him from the house;
We never spoke his name;
But all his trespass was our cross,
His ill-report our shame.

And if we saw him in the street,
We turned our heads aside;
And so it passed, until in rags
And poverty he died.

In life he could be none of ours;
But right is ever right.
He's buried with the family,
His faults turfed out of sight.

His grave is neat as any there;
On Saturdays we go
With roses in the summer-time,
And holly wreaths in snow.

And every Sunday praise the Lord
With calm and thankful brow,
That tidied and respectable,
We can own Richard now.

Ada Jackson

THE BIRD OF NIGHT

A shadow is floating through the moonlight.
Its wings don't make a sound.
Its claws are long, its beak is bright.
Its eyes try all the corners of the night.

It calls and calls: all the air swells and heaves
And washes up and down like water.
The ear that listens to the owl believes
In death. The bat beneath the eaves,

The mouse beside the stone are still as death.
The owl's air washes them like water.
The owl goes back and forth inside the night,
And the night holds its breath.

Randall Jarrell

THE YOUNG ONES

They slip on to the bus, hair piled up high.
New styles each month, it seems to me. I look,
Not wanting to be seen, casting my eye
Above the unread pages of a book.

They are fifteen or so. When I was thus,
I huddled in school coats, my satchel hung
Lop-sided on my shoulder. Without fuss
These enter adolescence; being young

Seems good to them, a state we cannot reach,
No talk of 'awkward ages' now. I see
How childish gazes staring out of each
Unfinished face prove me incredibly

Old-fashioned. Yet at least I have the chance
To size up several stages—young yet old,
Doing the twist, mocking an 'old-time' dance:
So many ways to be unsure or bold.

Elizabeth Jennings

WARNING TO PARENTS

Save them from terror; do not let them see
The ghost behind the stairs, the hidden crime.
They will, no doubt, grow out of this in time
And be impervious as you and me.

Be sure there is a night-light close at hand;
The plot of that old film may well come back,
The ceiling, with its long, uneven crack,
May hint at things no child can understand.

You do all this and are surprised one day
When you discover how the child can gloat
On Belsen and on tortures—things remote
To him. You find it hard to watch him play

With thoughts like these, and find it harder still
To think back to the time when you also
Caught from the cruel past a childish glow
And felt along your veins the wish to kill.

Fears are more personal than we had guessed—
We only need ourselves; time does the rest.

Elizabeth Jennings

THAW

Suddenly air is careless, generous,
caressing where it gripped. On lawns
the snowmen shrink to tiny pyramids
their eyes of frizzled coke roll out like tears
the blackbird launches song on running streams
and rising like a tide the grass
wells over snow and leaves it islanded
while hills like withheld waves tremble to move.

Time lives again. There are ripples, rivulets
in lanes and gutters, shimmers across bark;
stones and jutting tree-roots shine, while
the heart that through the rigid months became
a memory of spring, an easy yearning,
must be itself again, trembling, susceptible.

Brian Jones

COUNTING THE MAD

This one was put in a jacket,
This one was sent home,
This one was given bread and meat
But would eat none,
And this one cried No No No No
All day long.

This one looked at the window
As though it were a wall,
This one saw things that were not there,
This one things that were,
And this one cried No No No No
All day long.

This one thought himself a bird,
This one a dog,
And this one thought himself a man,
An ordinary man,
And cried and cried No No No No
All day long.

Donald Justice

JAPANESE FAN

Weak paper nerved
By thirty-three bamboo bones
Displayed like tendons or
Fingers, bird's wing stretched
Free in the fowler's hand.

Membrane folded upon
Yourself, half-opened, spread,
Flexing in easy joints
The cut air of the seasons,
Scents of musk and incense.

In dancing, you can be raised
Slowly, like a rolled blind of
Split bamboo, or lowered like
Moon among willows. Shut,
Stuck in the sash like a dagger.

Painted with one fish, a cucumber,
Two loquats or an ancient poem,
You are both book and signature,
Pages I close and open
On seal stamped red, a pen-name.

You both reveal and hide, indicate
Shock, shyness, sympathy, distress.
—Open or closed, you are
The eyes of the East,
The paper window of a soul.

Ningyo-cho

James Kirkup

FOUR HAIKU
ON THE INLAND SEA

Morning

Are clouds or mountains
Floating in the island air
Half sea, half heaven?

Spring

Our boat softly swims
In falling cherry petals.
The fresh spray is pink.

Autumn

Each drifting island
Leans its lonely pine, and red
Maples fan dark glens.

Evening

In the amber dusk
Each island dreams its own night.
The sea swarms with gold.

James Kirkup

SUMO WRESTLERS

If looks could kill,
These two hunks
Of sullen meat would long ago
Have eyed each other dead.

Bestowing on the fan-flocked air
Brief cascades of salt,
They stump slowly,
With studied boredom,
Into the ring of sand,
Huge flesh slopping,
Rumps and hams pocked and scarred
In black breechclouts.

Adjusting their bland bellies,
They arrange dainty hands
On the ground before them,
Crouch like grumpy toads.
But something tells them this
Is not the moment to engage.

They stretch up,
Tall in lacquered topknots,
And give each other long looks.
Contempt? No.
Intimidation? Perhaps.

Slowly lumber away
And leisurely return,
Spraying parabolas of tired salt
To purify the ring,
Propitiate the gods.

Crouched again, calm thighs
Spread, clash

Suddenly together
Push slap shove hook grunt heave
Buttressed against each other

Bare backsides cruppered
Black-belted bellies uddering
Paws groping for a girth-hold
Brute buttocks and bellies grappled
In shuddering embrace.

Till one is toppled,
Flopped like an avalanche,
Ten tons of rice-balls tumbling
Into a pleased ringside geisha's lap.

Asakusa: Kuramae Kokugikan

James Kirkup

EARTHQUAKE DREAM

Open your window on the high
Balcony whose frail white grate
Glows with geraniums against a sky
Of blue as soft as soot, and overhangs
The grand piano of the lake,
Dropping its coals of petals
That the winds of summer shake
With sudden bangs—

A sound of water
Dropping like stones
And with a clatter
Smashing the aspidistras in
The stunned courtyard.

The smattering of tiles
Drop past the window
Like grey snow.

The bed thumps down steps
And in the sequinned picture a nun
Frantically shakes her head at us
From the flaking wall.

We sit up in bed, and this
Makes the balcony outside
The creepered window rend
Its wrought-iron scrollwork
That with a smothered crash
Drops into a tree in a shower of
Blossom and birds.

After the balcony,
Our brass bed flops
Into the accommodating tree.

We lie there waiting for the firemen,
And staring up at the house-end that wears
Telephone wires like a tangled shawl.

Nagasaki

James Kirkup

THE AERIAL CONTORTIONIST

She must always remember
Not to start off on the wrong foot.

Widely smiling without a sound
In spangled tights she sits
High on the strumming wire.

She lifts—well, not just
A leg and a foot, but
Something that twines like
A root in the ground of air.

Her hands dispose it round her nape
Like a spangled boa.
Now her other leg she must take
And round the other shoulder
Nonchalantly drape.

Encouraging it like a pet
Snake; with here a slap and there
A pat, she writhes it,
Infinitely slowly, out and in
Beneath a dislocated chin.

The backs of her knees now clasp
Her armpits, while her feet
Somehow dangle in her lap
Where her heels
Perform unnumbered entrechats
Between her hands.
Upon which now
Her whole contrivance stands.

(Applause!)

She stares,
Widely smiling without a sound,
(But now the smile is upside-down)
At the ring's great O,
A mixed-up kid who cannot grow.

Do not ask me why
She does not eat
Her hat, nor how she will untie
That knot of meat.

Sendagaya: Bolshoi Circus

James Kirkup

NOT CRICKET

I hear continually on the lips of men
Who fought in wars, who slaved in prison camps
Of captors' cruelties, starvation, lingering death,
Of tortures, atrocities, inhuman rage.

We are all prisoners of one another,
And all our captors are ourselves.
We are all beasts. But beasts
Do not disgrace each other as do men.

I, too, remember brutal overseers
In the labour camps of Britain, men
Who could only relish power
If they could degrade, mock, punish

With violence as sad as any commandant's,
With anger that revealed the heart of war.
I remember also those who sheltered me,
Although they had no cause, and suffered for it.

I remember those in foreign camps
Who allowed themselves to love their captors,
And were loved. On both sides
A common brotherhood survived.

Not for us to rant of war's bad taste,
To issue pleas for decency, fair play.
If we permit our governments to arm for peace,
We sanction war, and must expect unpleasantnesses.

Hiroshima

James Kirkup

CENA

A crowded Last
Supper, thirteen heads,
Twenty-six hands, some
Under the table's
Long linenfold skirts,
Elbows getting in the way,
Feet in sandals kicked
Under the stout trestles,
Fingers dipped in dishes,
Breaking bread, carafe
Decanting acid wine,
Dark, muddy, poor stuff,
John, James Judas,
Even the betrayer
His face tanned by a golden halo
Turned all in profile
And the thirteen auras
All at different heights
Bob and jostle above
The tablecloth's white Jordan
Like balloons, buoys, mooring lights.

In mid-channel
One full face
In solitude.

James Kirkup

PLAINTIVE GEOMETRY

How happy the hostess who finds she can plan
A party including a notable man,
But let her beware of the grim mistake

That many a lady is prone to make
By thinking: 'If *one* Name's an asset, well then,
Why shouldn't I try to get *two* famous men?
    Each bathed in the glow that his equal bestows
    Is sure to start topping the other's bon mots.'

But joining two suns makes for total eclipse,
A notable failing of quotable quips
    Since each wants the limelight in *his* gin and tonic
    And, having to share it, turns dour and laconic.
At best, one celebrity falls asleep
While the other discusses his compost heap.
    As stated in Euclid's quaint conceit:
    Parallel lions can never meet.

Felicia Lamport

HISTORICAL SURVEY

It seems odd
  That whenever man chooses
To play God—
  God loses.

Felicia Lamport

→DRAWN ONWARD←

The learned men of Rome
Could turn a palindrome[1]
   But they were not the first,
For Adam, says the myth,
Began conversing with
   A sentence that reversed:

→'Mad*am* I'm Adam'← seemed
A phrase to be esteemed
   The moment it was popped
But that was not to be.
His lady instantly
   Said →'Eve'←, which left it topped.

Anonymous, that most
Prolific bard, can boast
   Of being host to this:
→'A man, a plan, a can-
Al, Panama!'← What span!
   What palindromic bliss!

I've wrung the alphabet
Repeatedly to get
   A Janus-phrase as spry
At backward somersaults,
But as each hope turns false
   →In words, alas, drown I←

Felicia Lamport

---

[1] → *Sator arepo teret opera rotas* ← which is translated as 'I cease from my work; the sower will wear away his wheels.' The thought is perhaps obscure and certainly difficult to slip into a conversation, but it should be noted that the original Latin forms a multiple anagram, with the initial letters of all the words spelling out the first word, the second letters spelling out the second word, and so on through all five.

AN ARUNDEL TOMB

Side by side, their faces blurred,
The earl and countess lie in stone,
Their proper habits vaguely shown
As jointed armour, stiffened pleat,
And that faint hint of the absurd—
The little dogs under their feet.

Such plainness of the pre-baroque
Hardly involves the eye, until
It meets his left-hand gauntlet, still
Clasped empty in the other; and
One sees, with a sharp tender shock,
His hand withdrawn, holding her hand.

They would not think to lie so long.
Such faithfulness in effigy
Was just a detail friends would see:
A sculptor's sweet commissioned grace
Thrown off in helping to prolong
The Latin names around the base.

They would not guess how early in
Their supine stationary voyage
The air would change to soundless damage,
Turn the old tenantry away;
How soon succeeding eyes begin
To look, not read. Rigidly they

Persisted, linked, through lengths and breadths
Of time. Snow fell, undated. Light
Each summer thronged the glass. A bright
Litter of birdcalls strewed the same
Bone-riddled ground. And up the paths
The endless altered people came,

Washing at their identity.
Now, helpless in the hollow of
An unarmorial age, a trough
Of smoke in slow suspended skeins
Above their scrap of history,
Only an attitude remains:

Time has transfigured them into
Untruth. The stone fidelity
They hardly meant has come to be
Their final blazon, and to prove
Our almost-instinct almost true:
What will survive of us is love.

Philip Larkin

MCMXIV

Those long uneven lines
Standing as patiently
As if they were stretched outside
The Oval or Villa Park,
The crowns of hats, the sun
On moustached archaic faces
Grinning as if it were all
An August Bank Holiday lark;

And the shut shops, the bleached
Established names on the sunblinds,
The farthings and sovereigns,
And dark-clothed children at play
Called after kings and queens,
The tin advertisements
For cocoa and twist, and the pubs
Wide open all day;

And the countryside not caring:
The place-names all hazed over
With flowering grasses, and fields
Shadowing Domesday lines
Under wheat's restless silence;
The differently-dressed servants
With tiny rooms in huge houses,
The dust behind limousines;

Never such innocence,
Never before or since,
As changed itself to past
Without a word—the men
Leaving the gardens tidy,
The thousands of marriages
Lasting a little while longer:
Never such innocence again.

Philip Larkin

TOADS REVISITED

Walking around in the park
Should feel better than work:
The lake, the sunshine,
The grass to lie on,

Blurred playground noises
Beyond black-stockinged nurses—
Not a bad place to be.
Yet it doesn't suit me,

Being one of the men
You meet of an afternoon:
Palsied old step-takers,
Hare-eyed clerks with the jitters,

Waxed-fleshed out-patients
Still vague from accidents,
And characters in long coats
Deep in the litter-baskets—

All dodging the toad work
By being stupid or weak.
Think of being them!
Hearing the hours chime,

Watching the bread delivered,
The sun by clouds covered,
The children going home;
Think of being them,

Turning over their failures
By some bed of lobelias,
Nowhere to go but indoors,
No friends but empty chairs—

No, give me my in-tray,
My loaf-haired secretary,
My shall-I-keep-the-call-in-Sir:
What else can I answer,

When the lights come on at four
At the end of another year?
Give me your arm, old toad;
Help me down Cemetery Road.

Philip Larkin

FISH AND WATER

A golden fish like a pint of wine
Rolls the sea undergreen,
Glassily balanced on the tide,
Only his skin between.

Fish and the water lean together
Separate and one;
Till a fatal flash of the instant sun
Lazily corkscrews down.

Did fish and water drink each other?
The reed leans there alone:
As we, who once drank each other's breath,
Have emptied the air and gone.

Laurie Lee

A BIRTHDAY CARD TO MY BEST FRIEND

This is the season when a few
    Dry leaves hang on dry wood,
When snow like peanut butter lies
    In streaks along the road,
When toes are etched by cold, and ears
    Throb in the icy air,
And only by induction we
    Know summer will recur.

Stretched out upon his bed your son
    Grows taller all night long.
The carol singers at the door
    Shuffle through their song.
Today's the day that you were born
    (How many years ago?)
They ring the bell: when they were born
    You were as bald as now.

Asleep upon another bed
   Your wife has ceased to grow;
Will bear (except for accidents)
   No further children now.
Cheek and belly sag with age;
   She's pains across her back;
Yet you must love her, since you've hung
   Three children round her neck.

Others will write the books you planned,
   Will stand for Parliament,
Make speeches, money, symphonies,
   Sculpt, cure, research, invent;
All you can do is tell your wife
   You love her greying hair,
Give sixpence to the carollers,
   And lend your son the car.

Laurence Lerner

TO SCHOOL

I sent my Muse to school:
   They taught her to walk straight,
To bear her body well,
   Scan, and alliterate.
So perfect was her poise
Men turned to watch her pass.

Skin deep, some said: those airs
   But fascinate the sight;
No true delight is hers.
   I thought, they must be right.
She plays a flawless part:
True verse is from the heart.

But when my heart was hurt,
  Too dumb to find relief,
She took voice till her art
  Sang the true shape of grief.
And the unschooled who heard
Loathed their own broken words.

Laurence Lerner

VULTURE

On ragged black sails
he soars hovering over
everything and death;
a blight in the eye
of the stunning sun.

An acquisitive droop
of beak, head and neck
dangles, dully angling,
a sentient pendulum
next to his keeled chest.

His eyes peer, piously
bloodless and hooded,
far-sighted, blighting
grasses, trees, hill-passes,
stones, streams, bones, bleached bones

with the tacky rags
of flesh adherent.
A slow ritual fold
of candid devil's palms
in blasphemous prayer—

the still wings sweep closed—
the hyaena of skies
plummets from the pulpit
of a tall boredom,
swallowing as he falls.

He brakes lazily
before his back breaks
to settle on two
creaky final wing-beats
flinging twin dust-winds.

He squats once fearfully.
Flushed with unhealthy plush
and pregustatory
satisfaction, head back,
he jumps lumpishly up.

Slack neck with the pecked
skin thinly shaking, he
sidles aside, then stumps
his deliberate banker's
gait to the stinking meal.

Douglas Livingstone

SUNSTRIKE

A solitary prospector
staggered, locked in a vision
of slate hills that capered
on the molten horizon.

Waterless, he came to where
a river had run, now a band
flowing only in ripples
of white unquenchable sand.

Cursing, he dug sporadically
here, here, as deep as his arm,
and sat quite still, eyes thirstily
incredulous on his palm.

A handful of alluvial
diamonds leered back, and more: mixed
in the scar, glinted globules
of rubies, emeralds, onyx.

And then he was swimming in fire
and drinking, splashing hot halos
of glittering drops at the choir
of assembled carrion crows.

Douglas Livingstone

PROFESSOR TUHOLSKY'S FACTS

Once upon a little planet,
A nice provincial planet set
Deep in the galactic sticks,
There lived an interesting thing
Called Man.

Man had two legs and two
Convictions: one he called Luck,
Which he believed in when things went right;
The other one he used when things went wrong.
This was called Religion.

Man was vertebrate, bipodic,
Omnivorously dieted, often bald,
And had a soul that never died.[1]
Also he had his fellow countrymen
To stop him getting over-confident.

Man ate a lot;
Plants, fish, animals, birds, snails . . .
Almost anything that he could reach;
Occasionally he ate other men,
But this was rare.

Each man had a liver,
A heart, a brain, and a flag.
These were his vital organs.
On these his life depended.
Doubtless there were men alive

With only half a liver,
Some had no heart,
And many had no brain.
But a man without a flag?
Impossible.

Man was the most useful living creature;
He raised the value of steel-shares;
Cheerfully he died a soldier's death,
Or committed spectacular crimes,
Thereby selling innumerable newspapers,

All of which have now vanished.

---

[1] Although extensive inter-galactic expeditions have searched the whole universe for what must be a colony of some trillion Immortal Souls, none have been found. And, in justice to these expeditions, it must be said that Man was known to tell lies about himself.

Many admired human character,
But it was split. One half was known as Male—
And did not want to think;
The other was called Female—
In whom thinking was discouraged.

Yet both had this in common:
They were full of fear.
They were afraid of cancer, debt,
Old-age, loneliness, and failure;
But most of all they feared their fellow man.
Thus justifying the name 'Sapiens'.

Man was Political.
He lived in groups.
Each group detested the next group.
O, there were so many detestations!
And the chief of these was called Patriotism.

Although he had two ears
Man rarely listened, and, if he did,
He only liked to hear promises, estimates
Of his own value, congratulations, and,
Above all, expressions of gratitude.
Of course, some men were different . . .
Thinkers, revolutionaries, saints,
But these were few,
And they were quickly crucified,
Shot, or poisoned.

And in addition to men there were
White South Africans, though,
As their extinction was hourly expected,
And did eventually arrive,
None of their artifacts survive.

Next week we study Dogs.

Christopher Logue

THE BARBARIAN INVASIONS

From distant Gaul the generals wrote how grave
Was the new threat; the common soldiers found
That they had lost the knack of being brave,

With every gap in harness made a wound
By thought. And waiting to be crossed,
There lay the frozen Rhine, and all the ground

Was hard and ringing with the iron frost.

Edward Lucie-Smith

THE WITNESSES

Dogs to their vomit, crows to carrion,
We keep on going back—this film, this play,
Personal histories, newspaper reports
About some trial over the North Sea—
Belsen and Auschwitz call for no passports,
Dachau is native ground for everyone.

Hard to forget a skill when once it's learned;
We know how to break bodies, how to break
The watch-spring of the will, and murder comes
A little easier, even by mistake;
The military spokesmen blame the times
More glibly than before the ovens burned.

Pain has its jargon: first *Arbeit macht frei*,
And now, perhaps, *Died trying to escape*—
Each phrase a lie that all the same is true,
Till words themselves lose substance, weight and shape;
When language lessens, we must also grow
As crude and mean and small as what we say.

Agreed one finds harsh tales in history books,
With here a woodcut—executioners
Busy about some quaintly bloody task;
Our fathers felt it no concern of theirs,
And formerly the scholars wrote quite brisk
Verdicts on iron maidens, thumbscrews, racks.

Now things are different. Voices fill my head.
'Men are like this,' they say. 'Are you like this?'
My father and my grandfather would not
Have understood; to me the question is
Simple and hard. Always within earshot
Stand there to judge us those six million dead.

Edward Lucie-Smith

SALISBURY PLAIN

Their heads bent down before the polar wind
From ridge to ridge two labourers cross the plough,
Smoke from a bonfire creeps along the ground,
Saplings and hedgerows tangled in its flow.

And fifty miles away the Channel gale
Beats in the bays; with loud metallic cries,
Wings spread and rigid, seagulls turn and sail
Sideways to leeward, fly as paper flies.

With furrows for the waves of a brown sea
The land heaves up, and tries to change its form;
Leaves fallen rise like spindrift, and the storm
Roars about forts and barrows which have stood
Three thousand years; it batters in the wood
As if to overthrow the Druids' tree.

Edward Lucie-Smith

BEDTIME STORY

Long long ago when the world was a wild place
Planted with bushes and peopled by apes, our
Mission Brigade was at work in the jungle.
    Hard by the Congo

Once, when a foraging detail was active
Scouting for green-fly, it came on a grey man, the
Last living man, in the branch of a baobab
    Stalking a monkey.

Earlier men had disposed of, for pleasure,
Creatures whose names we scarcely remember—
Zebra, rhinoceros, elephants, wart-hog,
    Lion, rats, deer. But

After the wars had extinguished the cities
Only the wild ones were left, half-naked
Near the Equator: and here was the last one,
    Starved for a monkey.

By then the Mission Brigade had encountered
Hundreds of such men; and their procedure,
History tells us, was only to feed them:
    Find them and feed them;

Those were the orders. And this was the last one.
Nobody knew that he was, but he was. Mud
Caked on his flat grey flanks. He was crouched, half-
    armed with a shaved spear

Glinting beneath broad leaves. When their jaws cut
Swathes through the bark and he saw fine teeth shine,
Round eyes roll round and forked arms waver
    Huge as the rough trunks

Over his head, he was frightened. Our workers
Marched through the Congo before he was born, but
This was the first time perhaps that he'd seen one.
      Staring in hot still

Silence, he crouched there: then jumped. With a long swing
Down from his branch, he had angled his spear too
Quickly, before they could hold him, and hurled it
      Hard at the soldier

Leading the detail. How could he know Queen's
Orders were only to help him? The soldier
Winced when the tipped spear pricked him. Unsheathing his
      Sting was a reflex.

Later the Queen was informed. There were no more
Men. An impetuous soldier had killed off,
Purely by chance, the penultimate primate.
      When she was certain,

Squadrons of workers were fanned through the Congo
Detailed to bring back the man's picked bones to be
Sealed in the archives in amber. I'm quite sure
      Nobody found them

After the most industrious search, though.
Where had the bones gone? Over the earth, dear,
Ground by the teeth of the termites, blown by the
      Wind, like the dodo's.

George MacBeth

BATS

have no accidents. They loop
their incredible horse-shoe
loops, dead-stop

on air-brakes,
road-safe on
squeaks: racketeering

their SOS noise in a
jai-alai
bat-jam

of collapsed umbrellas, a
Chancery Lane
of avoided

collisions, all in a
cave without lights: then
hung

happy, a snore
of strap-hangers
undergrounding

without an *Evening
Standard* between them
to the common Waterloo

that awaits bats, like
all beasts, then
off now, zoom!

Man, you can't even
hear them, bats,
are they?

George MacBeth

THE RED HERRING

after Cros

There was once a high wall, a bare wall. And
against this wall, there was a ladder,
a long ladder. And on the ground,
under the ladder, there was a red
herring. A dry red herring.

And then a man came along. And in his hands
(they were dirty hands) this man had
a heavy hammer, a long nail
(it was also a sharp nail) and
a ball of string. A thick ball of string.

All right. So the man climbed up
the ladder (right up to the top)
and knocked in the sharp nail:
spluk! Just like that.
Right on top of the wall. The bare wall.

Then he dropped the hammer. It dropped
right down to the ground. And onto the nail
he tied a piece of string, a long
piece of string, and onto the string
he tied the red herring. The dry red herring.

And let it drop. And then he climbed
down the ladder (right down
to the bottom), picked up the hammer
and also the ladder (which was pretty heavy)
and went off. A long way off.

And since then, that red herring, the dry
red herring on the end of the string, which is
quite a long piece, has been

very very slowly swinging and
swinging to a stop. A full stop.

I expect you wonder why I made
up this story, such a simple story. Well,
I did it just to annoy people.
Serious people. And perhaps also
to amuse children. Small children.

George MacBeth

FROGS

Frogs sit more solid
Than anything sits. In mid-leap they are
Parachutists falling
In a free fall. They die on roads
With arms across their chests and
Heads high.

I love frogs that sit
Like Buddha, that fall without
Parachutes, that die
Like Italian tenors.

Above all, I love them because,
Pursued in water, they never
Panic so much that they fail
To make stylish triangles
With their ballet dancer's
Legs.

Norman MacCaig

SOLITARY CROW

Why solitary crow? He in his feathers
Is a whole world of crow—of a dry-stick nest,
Of windy distances where to be crow is best,
Of tough-guy clowning and of black things done
To a sprawled lamb whose blood beads in the sun.

Sardonic anarchist. Where he goes he carries,
Since there's no centre, what a centre is,
And that is crow, the ragged self that's his.
Smudged on a cloud, he jeers at the world then halts
To jeer at himself and turns two somersaults.

He ambles through the air, flops down and seesaws
On a blunt fencepost, hiccups and says Caw.
The sun glints greasy on his working craw
And adds a silver spot to that round eye
Whose black light bends and cocks the world awry.

Norman MacCaig

STARLINGS

Can you keep it so,
cool tree, making a blue cage
for an obstreperous population?—
for a congregation of mediaeval scholars
quarrelling in several languages?—
for busybodies marketing
in the bazaar of green leaves?—
for clockwork fossils that can't be still even
when the Spring runs down?

No tree, no blue cage can contain
that restlessness. They whirr off
and sow themselves in a scattered handful
on the grass—and are
bustling monks
tilling their green precincts.

Norman MacCaig

CROSSING THE BORDER

I sit with my back to the engine, watching
the landscape pouring away out of my eyes.
I think I know where I'm going and have
some choice in the matter.

I think, too, that this was a country
of bog-trotters, moss-troopers,
fired ricks and rooftrees in the black night—glinting
on tossed horns and red blades.
I think of lives
bubbling into the harsh grass.

What difference now?
I sit with my back to the future, watching
time pouring away into the past. I sit, being helplessly
lugged backwards
through the Debatable Lands of history, listening
to the execrations, the scattered cries, the
falling of rooftrees
in the lamentable dark.

Norman MacCaig

JUST AN OLD SWEET SONG

The pale, drooping girl and the swaggering soldier,
The row-dow-dow-dow of the stuttering drum,
The bugles, the charges, the swords are romantic
For those who survive when the bugles are dumb.

The lice of the trenches, the mortars, machine-guns,
The prisoners exchanged and the Christmas Day lull,
The no-man's-land raid and the swagger-stick rally
Are stirring, for when was a finished war dull?

The road-block, the ambush, the scrap on the mountain,
The slouch-hat, the trench-coat, the raid in the night,
The hand-grenade hefted, police-barracks burning,
Ah, that was the life, and who's hurt in a fight?

The blitzkreig, the landings, the victories, the losses,
The eyes blind with sand, the retreat, the alert,
Commando and D-Day, H-Hour and Block-buster
Have filed through the glass, and was anyone hurt?

A flash and a mushroom, a hole in the planet,
Strange growth in the flora, less fauna to feed,
Peace enters, the silence returns and the waters
Advance on the earth as the war tides recede.

Donagh MacDonagh

MY WICKED UNCLE

It was my first funeral.
Some loss of status as a nephew since
Dictates that I recall
My numbness, my grandfather's hesitance,
My five aunts busy in the hall.

I found him closeted with living souls—
Coffined to perfection in the bedroom.
Death had deprived him of his mustache,
His thick horn-rimmed spectacles,
The easy corners of his salesman dash
(Those things by which I had remembered him)
And sundered him behind unnatural gauze.
His hair was badly parted on the right
As if for Sunday school. That night
I saw my uncle as he really was.

The narrative he dispensed was mostly
Wicked avuncular fantasy—
He went in for waistcoats and haircream.
But something about him
Demanded that you picture the surprise
Of the chairman of the board, when to
'What will you have with your whiskey?' my uncle
   replies—
'Another whiskey, please.'

Once he was jailed in New York
Twice on the same day—
The crookedest chief steward in the Head Line.
And once (he affected communism)
He brought the whole crew out on strike
In protest at the loss of a day's pay
Crossing the international date line.

They buried him slowly above the sea,
The young Presbyterian minister
Rumpled and windy in the sea air.
A most absorbing ceremony—
Ashes to ashes, dust to dust.
I saw sheep huddled in the long wet grass
Of the golf-course, and the empty freighters
Sailing for ever down Belfast Lough

In a fine rain, their sirens going,
As the gradual graph of my uncle's life and
Times dipped precipitately
Into the bowels of Carnmoney Cemetery.

His teenage kids are growing horns and claws—
More wicked already than ever my uncle was.

Derek Mahon

CHRISTMAS SONNETS
For Pat St John

I

SANTA CLAUS

His sullen kinsmen, by the winter sea,
Said he was holy: then, to his surprise,
They stripped him, flayed him, tied him to a tree,
Sliced off his tongue, and burnt out both his eyes.

The trampling reindeer smelt him where he lay,
Blood dyeing his pelt, his beard white with rime,
Until he lurched erect and limped away,
Winter on winter, forward into time.

Then to new houses squat in brick he came
And heard the children's birdlike voices soar
In three soft syllables: they called his name.

The chimney shook: the children in surprise
Stared up as their invited visitor
Lifted his claws above them, holes for eyes.

Dom Moraes

FAMILY DINNER

The spraddled turkey waited for the knife.
The scything holly clashed: the pleading peal
Of bells swung Christ back on a horny heel
To clutch the cross like a desired wife.

And now, pinned there, he flutters till they come,
The gross men and the women they are with,
Who kneel and take his soft flesh in their teeth,
And, chewing the holy cud, flock slowly home.

There as the golden children gather by,
Hung with chill bells, the harsh tree is displayed:
A delicate fear wets each child's eye

While the gross father, with the whisky flush
Deepening in his cheeks, prepares the blade
To pare off from the bone the warm white flesh.

Dom Moraes

THE CWM ABOVE PENRHIWCEIBER

There was sparkling water, too small
For a river, too big for a stream.
As boys we sampled it as early
As April when the weather changed.
We dammed it and dived off a tree
And gasped in the trout-cold water.
We crept through dark growth
Of young and old trees, tall
Fern and tangled bramble where the sun

Could only get fingers through.
The ground sagged under foot
And bird and insect silence
Was rich with arrows of history.
Ghosts sighed in a trapped
Breeze and every indigo shadow
Hid a skeleton and a sword.
Out in the sunlight we shouted
Our fears away and romped home,
Glancing back at our Cwm
Now buried under rubbish from pits.

Robert Morgan

LOW SEAM MINER

He returns day after day
To crouch on knees and side
In a seam two feet high
With a patch of cold light
Making a hole in darkness
Where the roof bends bleeding posts
Above his tilted head.
His tense hands curled on a shaft
Stab in slow arcs over the coal.
He works . . . and listens to the roof and floor
Straining to close the gap where he lies.
Yet he returns day after day
Unafraid to his bleak cell.

Robert Morgan

HUW'S FARM

Up at Huw's farm nature
Is invading gently, fingering
Its way over a wilderness of deserted
Relics. Here, Huw, Rachel
And two sons once toiled
On a bare hill blotted
With cones of slag and memories.
Now shattered windows grin
Under creeping green locks
And the rude wind mocks
The empty rooms inhabited
By the curious sad silence of
Vanished people and homely residue.
Out in the brambled yard a rust
Crippled plough is sinking into
Forgotten soil and a toppled
Dry wall lets in the tide of
Couch grass from the hill breast.
Down in the valley, pits,
Vague through dust and smoke,
Whisper the dark fugue of
Industry and stubborn faith
Under a chapel eye of God.

Robert Morgan

DROIT DE SEIGNEUR
1820

In a grey rectory a clergyman was reading
Fortunate by firelight the *Connaught Journal*.
The shutters were closed, for famine was spreading
Among the people. The portrait of Cromwell,

One hand on the Bible, the other on a sword,
Had been stowed that evening under a haystack.
The air was crackling with the whips of rhetoric.

A groom was saddling his mare in the stable
While a redcoat stumbled down the loft ladder
Buttoning his tunic, followed by a girl
Who ran to the kitchen. The yard lantern
Yellowed the stirrups and the buckled leather
On the mare's girth as he combed her down.
The master was for hunting the Ribbonmen:

A secret band, swearing oaths by moonlight,
Refusing to pay tithes or rent to the landlord,
Who battered on lonely doors after midnight,
And wore round their sleeves a white riband.
He called it his duty to commit these rogues
To the jury of gentlemen at Galway Assizes.
Saving of property went with saving of souls.

So he galloped out with a few soldiers
On to the gravelled road under the lime-trees
With his father's pistol in a handsome holster.
They ambushed a wedding from the next parish.
All escaped except a young simpleton
In whose pocket they found a white bandage.
Twenty miles to Galway he was marched in chains.

In the pigeon park the heifers were grazing
Under the beech-trees. The soldiers had gone.
Behind the frown of the windows, browsing
On the price of cattle in the *Connaught Journal*,
The rector looked out on the frost and the sun.
The girl ran across the yard with a bucket.
'Tomorrow,' he read, 'the boy will be executed.'

Richard Murphy

A SPELL BEFORE WINTER

After the red leaf and the gold have gone,
Brought down by the wind, then by hammering rain
Bruised and discoloured, when October's flame
Goes blue to guttering in the cusp, this land
Sinks deeper into silence, darker into shade.
There is a knowledge in the look of things,
The old hills hunch before the north wind blows.

Now I can see certain simplicities
In the darkening rust and tarnish of the time,
And say over the certain simplicities,
The running water and the standing stone,
The yellow haze of the willow and the black
Smoke of the elm, the silver, silent light
Where suddenly, readying toward nightfall,
The sumac's candelabrum darkly flames.
And I speak to you now with the land's voice,
It is the cold, wild land that says to you
A knowledge glimmers in the sleep of things:
The old hills hunch before the north wind blows.

Howard Nemerov

THE COMPANIONS

There used to be gods in everything, and now they've
  gone.
A small one I remember, in a green-gray stone,
Would watch me go by with his still eyes of a toad,
And in the branch of an elm that hung across the road
Another was; he creaked at me on windless days.
Now that he's gone I think he might have wanted praise
For trying to speak my language and getting that far at
  least
Along on the imitation of a speaking beast.

Maybe he wanted help, maybe they all cried out
As they could, or stared helpless to enter into thought
With 'read me,' 'answer me,' or 'teach me how to be
Whatever I am, and in return for teaching me
I'll tell you what I was in you, how greater far
Than I are seeking you in fountain, sun, and star.'
That's but interpretation, the deep folly of man
To think that things can squeak at him more than things
    can.

And yet there came those voices up out of the ground
And got into my head, until articulate sound
Might speak them to themselves. We went a certain way
Together on that road, and then I turned away.

I must have done, I guess, to have grown so abstract
That all the lonely summer night's become but fact,
That when the cricket signals I no longer listen,
Nor read the glowworms' constellations when they glisten.

Howard Nemerov

GRACE TO BE SAID AT THE
SUPERMARKET

That God of ours, the Great Geometer,
Does something for us here, where He hath put
(if you want to put it that way) things in shape,
Compressing the little lambs in orderly cubes,
Making the roast a decent cylinder,
Fairing the tin ellipsoid of a ham,
Getting the luncheon meat anonymous
In squares and oblongs with the edges bevelled
Or rounded (streamlined, maybe, for greater speed).

Praise Him, He hath conferred aesthetic distance
Upon our appetites, and on the bloody
Mess of our birthright, our unseemly need,
Imposed significant form. Through Him the brutes
Enter the pure Euclidean kingdom of number,
Free of their bulging and blood-swollen lives
They come to us holy, in cellophane
Tranparencies, in the mystical body,

That we may look unflinchingly on death
As the greatest good, like a philosopher should.

Howard Nemerov

SPEECH DAY

The girls of the County Mod
Are taught to believe in God,
Team spirit, examination,
And the value of Education.

Tonight, when speeches are made,
The usual things are said
To promote in the children zest
For what their elders think best.

As always, Alderman Mason
On this auspicious occasion
Sums up with his proclamation:
'There's nowt like a good ejoocaashun.'

As the headmistress rises
And the girls go up for their prizes
One wonders what Time will do
To this hopeful retinue—

These pink-cheeked dears who stand
Glimpsing the promised land,
Life like a motor-boat humming
And Christmas undoubtedly coming.

At typewriter, loom or till
Most of these lasses will
Mark time until they are wed;
Jane in a year will be dead;

Sally is destined to be
Unmarried mother of three ...
Only Rose, of the shining lights,
Will attain the topmost heights.

Even Rose will sometimes ask,
At her magisterial desk
In another class-room, 'Mason,
Were you right about education?'

May envy the never-dids
Who graduated through palais,
Coffee-bar, bowling-alley,
To husband, home, and kids.

Francis Newbold

THE ELVERS

An iron pipe
Syphoning gallons of brine
From the hundred foot below sea-level mine—
A spring salty as mussels,
Bilberry-stained with ore;

And the pink, dry-paper thrift rustles
In the draught made by the spray
As the pumps thrust the water upward
To a rock-locked bay.

And, quick in the brown burn,
Black whips that flick and shake,
Live darning-needles with big-eye heads—
Five-inch elvers
That for twice five seasons snake
Through the earth's turn and return of water
To seep with the swell into rifts of the old workings
And be churned out on cinder beds and fern.

The pumps pour on;
The elvers shimmy in the weed. And I,
Beneath my parochial complement of sky,
Plot their way
From Sargasso Sea to Cumberland,
From tide to pit,
Knowing the why of it
No more than they.

Norman Nicholson

THE COCK'S NEST

The spring my father died—it was winter, really,
February fill-grave, but March was in
By the time we felt the bruise of it and knew
How empty the rooms were—that spring
A wren flew to our yard, over Walter Willson's
Warehouse roof and the girls' school playground
From the old allotments that are now no more than a
   compost

For raising dockens and cats. It found a niche
Tucked behind the pipe of the bathroom outflow,
Caged in a wickerwork of creeper; then
Began to build:
Three times a minute, hour after hour,
Backward and forward to the backyard wall,
Nipping off neb-fulls of the soot-spored moss
Rooted between the bricks. In a few days
The nest was finished. They say the cock
Leases an option of sites and leaves the hen
To choose which nest she will. She didn't choose our yard.
And as March gambolled out, the fat King-Alfred sun
Blared down too early from its tinny trumpet
On new-dug potato-beds, the still bare creeper,
The cock's nest with never an egg in,
And my father dead.

Norman Nicholson

ON THE CLOSING OF MILLOM
IRONWORKS: SEPTEMBER 1968

Wandering by the heave of the town park, wondering
Which way the day will drift,
On the spur of a habit I turn to the feathered
Weathercock of the furnace chimneys.

                But no grey smoke-tail
Pointers the mood of the wind. The hum
And blare that for a hundred years
Drummed at the town's deaf ears,
Now fills the air with the roar of its silence.
They'll need no more to swill the slag-dust off the
    windows;
The curtains will be cleaner
And the grass plots greener
Round the Old Folks' council flats. The tanged autumnal
    mist

Is filtered free of soot and sulphur,
And the wind blows in untainted.
It's beautiful to breathe the sharp night air.
And, look, scrawled on the walls of the Working Men's:
'No-one starves in the Welfare State.'
                                        They stand
By the churchyard gate,
Hands in pockets, shoulders to the slag,
The men whose fathers stood there back in '28,
When their sons were at school with me.
                                        The town
Rolls round the century's bleak orbit.
                                        Down
On the ebb-tide sands, the five-funnelled
Battleship of the furnaces lies beached and rusting;
Run aground, not foundered;
Not a crack in her hull;
Lacking but a loan to float her off.
                                        The Market
Square is busy as the men file by
To sign on at the 'Brew'. But not a face
Tilts upward, no-one enquires of the sky.
The smoke prognosticates no how
Or why of any practical tomorrow.
For what does it matter if it rains all day?
And what's the good of knowing
Which way the wind is blowing
When whichever way it blows it's a cold wind now?

Norman Nicholson

HAVE YOU BEEN TO LONDON?

'Have you been to London?'
My grandmother asked me.
      'No.'—
China dogs on the mantelshelf,
Paper blinds at the window,
Three generations simmering on the bright black lead,
And a kettle filled to the neb,
Spilled over long ago.

I blew into the room, threw
My scholarship cap on the rack,
Wafted visitors up the flue
With the draught of my coming in—
Ready for Saturday's mint imperials,
Ready to read
The serial in *Titbits*, the evangelical
Tale in the parish magazine,
Under the green
Glare of the gas,
Under the stare of my grandmother's Queen.

My grandmother burnished her sleek steel hair—
Not a tooth in her jaw,
Nor alphabet in her head,
Her spectacles lost before I was born,
Her lame leg stiff in the sofa corner,
Her crutch at the steady:
'They shut doors after them
In London,' she said.

I crossed the hearth and thumped the door to,
Then turned to Saturday's stint,
My virtuosity of print
And grandmother's wonder:
Reading of throttler and curate,

Blood, hallelujahs and thunder,
While the generations boiled down to one
And the kettle burnt dry
In a soon grandmotherless room,

Reading for forty years,
Till the print swirled out like a down-catch of soot
And the wind howled round
A world left cold and draughty,
Un-latched, un-done,
By all the little literate boys
Who hadn't been to London.

Norman Nicholson

A LOCAL PREACHER'S GOODBYE

'I'll meet you again up there'—
He pointed to the smoke
With black umbrella finger
(The chimneys tall as hymns,
Fuming with extemporary prayer)—
'I'll see you all up there,'
He said.

Six boys or seven
In the dark October drizzle,
Class tickets in our pockets,
Ready to leave Heaven
Locked in with the hymn-books;
Supper and bed
Hard on by the Market Clock—
'Good night, Mr Fawcett, sir,'
We said.

Forty years of soot and rain;
A Bible-insured
Ghost of chapel steward
And manufacturer of aerated waters,
With grey-ginger beard
Bubbling my unwritten poetry—
'Grand seeing you again!'
I'll say,
I often say.

Norman Nicholson

SPLENDID GIRLS

Those splendid girls at the wheels of powerful cars,
Sheer mechanism setting off slender charms.
I glimpse daredevil smiles as they whip past.

What are they all eager for, driving so fast
That I see them only momentarily? They are
Wholly desirable for half a heart-beat.

They have such style, such red nails! They are so neat!
But though they appear to drive at a dangerous speed
They do not do anything at random, that's for sure.

So keep your shirt on, they are spoken for.
They are as bright and lively as advertisements
For cigarettes or petrol or soap.

But there is no danger, and there is no hope.
Those reckless smiles have been carefully painted.
They are that sort of doll.

Everything, but everything, is under control.

John Normanton

THE MONSTER WHO LOVED THE HERO

I met a monster in a wood:
'It's not my fault!' choked through her cries,
Blowing her blue nose loud as she could,
Tears pouring from her bloodshot eyes.

Being practised in the art,
I raised my lance to poke her through;
But I could not play out my part—
Hers was no strategy I knew.

'The ugliest need love the most,
And if you take me home with you,
You'll find, at last, someone to trust,
For Beauty never could be true.'

Such fine sentiment made me pause,
Though she was not my type one bit;
It seemed against my whole life's cause
To find love and not pity it.

She saw me weaken, and she smiled.
I swear she gloated in her grin.
I must confess that got me riled:
I took my lance and did her in.

Robert Pack

THE MINERS

Out of the dark mouth they came—
all but one—lifted like Lazarus,
but looking like bearded tourists visiting
a cave, with a strained smile for the cameras.

Throughout the more than twenty days
of night, they had talked, they said, baseball,
exhausting the batting averages of both major
leagues, and showing children by matchlight.

And had heard through the walled stone a faint
scratching, and a distant sound, high-pitched
and strange, like the sound that bats make
when hurt, or a child's voice crying.

The drills broke on the rock. The body
was not retrieved, and lies there still
curled in its tight black room
so casually and efficiently a grave.

They must dream of him sometimes—the one
who was not saved, and turning in sleep
strike the sharp-faced rock, and awake—
staring into the blackness of a tomb.

Paul Petrie

CUT

For Susan O'Neill Roe

What a thrill—
My thumb instead of an onion.
The top quite gone
Except for a sort of a hinge

Of skin,
A flap like a hat,
Dead white.
Then that red plush.

Little pilgrim,
The Indian's axed your scalp.
Your turkey wattle
Carpet rolls

Straight from the heart.
I step on it,
Clutching my bottle
Of pink fizz.

A celebration, this is.
Out of a gap
A million soldiers run,
Redcoats, every one.

Whose side are they on?
O my
Homunculus, I am ill.
I have taken a pill to kill

The thin
Papery feeling.
Saboteur,
Kamikaze man—

The stain on your
Gauze Ku Klux Klan
Babushka
Darkens and tarnishes and when

The balled
Pulp of your heart
Confronts its small
Mill of silence

How you jump—
Trepanned veteran,
Dirty girl,
Thumb stump.

Sylvia Plath

SNAKECHARMER

As the gods began one world, and man another,
So the snakecharmer begins a snáky sphere
With moon-eye, mouth-pipe. He pipes. Pipes green. Pipes
water.

Pipes water green until green waters waver
With reedy lengths and necks and undulatings.
And as his notes twine green, the green river

Shapes its images around his songs.
He pipes a place to stand on, but no rocks,
No floor: a wave of flickering grass tongues

Supports his foot. He pipes a world of snakes,
Of sways and coilings, from the snake-rooted bottom
Of his mind. And now nothing but snakes

Is visible. The snake-scales have become
Leaf, become eyelid; snake-bodies, bough, breast
Of tree and human. And he within this snakedom

Rules the writhings which make manifest
His snakehood and his might with pliant tunes
From his thin pipe. Out of this green nest

As out of Eden's navel twist the lines
Of snaky generations: let there be snakes!
And snakes there were, are, will be—till yawns

Consume this piper and he tires of music
And pipes the world back to the simple fabric
Of snake-warp, snake-weft. Pipes the cloth of snakes

To a melting of green waters, till no snake
Shows its head, and those green waters back to
Water, to green, to nothing like a snake.
Puts up his pipe, and lids his moony eye.

Sylvia Plath

MRS MIDDLEDITCH

Fitting a thin glove
Over a dry hand,
Over a gold ring (plain
As the nine-carat love
Of her good man now dead),
Mrs Middleditch pats
For the sake of tidiness
The back of her tidy head.

'It's time for shopping again.
I must think of the things I need,
Or *think* I need. Time
To go out. If I stay in
I mightn't go out at all.
I might give way to doubt
And ask, What *is* it all *for?*
And not go out of my door:

'And think, Why leave my bed
To wash and dress and eat,
And wash up, and wash out a dress,
And dress up, and go out to tea?
Sameness of fading days,
Is this what life should be?
Am I the slightest use?
And who would ever miss *me?*

'I must make out a list,
I suppose a widow must eat:
A caterpillar must eat—
But then, it can hope for wings.
Floor polish, cocoa, cake,
Sago, margarine, yeast—
A gruesome menu there
For my lonesome evening feast!'

'Oh, Mrs Middleditch, good
Morning to you!'
                    'And to you!'
'A lovely morning again!'
'It is. (But you give me a pain;
What goes on in my head
You neither care nor guess;
One can have a little too much
Bright neighbourliness.)'

At the Supermarket door
An amplifier hails
Each housewife—and her purse—
With smooth false bonhomie.
Could anything be worse?
Mrs Middleditch hears
With a shiver of distaste
These words affront her ears:

'A Supermorning, madam,
For Supermarketing!
Our cut-price Superfoods
Are best for each and all,
Our Supergoods await you
On every Supershelf,
So take a Superbasket
And help your Superself!'

'Oh, Mrs Middleditch,
This place *is* a boon!
I've come here for everything
Since my honeymoon.'
'Yes, yes, convenient,
Marvellous, I agree—
And yet I feel somehow as if
It's pressing in on me:

'There's too much of everything,
Too much advertisement.
I ask myself if what is said
Is ever what is meant—
FISH FLAKES *taste breezy*,
CAKE FIX *bakes lightest*,
QUICK WAX *makes work easy*,
SQUELCH *whitens whites whitest*.'

'Oh, Mrs Middleditch,
Excuse me if I ask it.
But you've not got a single thing
So far in your Superbasket!
Let me recommend these peaches
And the nice thick double cream,
And you'll find the chicken breasts
(Milk-fed, of course) a dream.'

'I've got a list of things I need
Or thought I needed. Now I know
That peaches, chickens, cream,
And even sago, cocoa, yeast,
Are things I cannot buy today.
Today I fast, not feast.
I can't put out my hand, I find
A double vision in my mind.

'Beyond abundance—butter, eggs,
Strength-giving meat and cubes of cheese,
And cylinders of beans and peas
And syrup-swimming halves of pears—
Deserts I see, and frowsty rags,
And groups of persons wearing these,
Bowed by the weight of nothingness;
I recognize them—refugees.

'I see a child with seething flies
Fouling its big, unblinking eyes,
Eyes fixed on me: a swollen child
With dangling, thin, rachitic wrists,
Listless and silent, watching me,
In want and in unwantedness
Waiting to learn why it was born—
While I draw up my shopping lists.

'It will not do! I have no appetite
For food. And none for charity!
Dull, shiftless outcasts under static skies,
They are myself. Only the pelican
That tore her breast could teach me how
To reach that place, to staunch with work
That open sore, to feed with love
One orphan fed upon by flies.'

'Oh Mrs Middleditch! Are you all right?'
Her answer was a sudden moan
And down she slumped upon the Superfloor,
The spotless floor of Non-Slip Superstone.
Inside her Superbasket was her head,
Unconscious prisoner of a Supercage.
'Quick, call the manager!' 'She was acting strange.'
'Silly old fool! she's reached the awkward age.'

William Plomer

BEFORE THE CRASH

Caught sight of from the car
(Just before the crash)
On the river bank
    Against a hanging cliff of bronze
    A great white colony
    Of resting and of nesting swans.

In marble attitudes
(Distant, as things are
Living their own lives)
    The swans, arranged in twos and threes,
    Were doing nothing; we
    Were doing eighty—and with ease.

Seen also from the car,
Minutes and miles along,
Flames in a ballet, stretch
    Enormous up from straw and trash
    In frenzy to attain
    The coda—just a little ash.

Tempi of swans and fires,
Cars, and suns beyond
Furnace-roaring suns
    No man will ever hear—in space
    These harmonize, none are
    Winners or losers in a race.

William Plomer

YOUR ATTENTION PLEASE

The Polar DEW has just warned that
A nuclear rocket strike of
At least one thousand megatons
Has been launched by the enemy
Directly at our major cities.
This announcement will take
Two and a quarter minutes to make,
You therefore have a further
Eight and a quarter minutes
To comply with the shelter

Requirements published in the Civil
Defence Code—section Atomic Attack.
A specially shortened Mass
Will be broadcast at the end
Of this announcement—
Protestant and Jewish services
Will begin simultaneously—
Select your wavelength immediately
According to instructions
In the Defence Code. Do not
Take well-loved pets (including birds)
Into your shelter—they will consume
Fresh air. Leave the old and bed-
ridden, you can do nothing for them.
Remember to press the sealing
Switch when everyone is in
The shelter. Set the radiation
Aerial, turn on the geiger barometer.
Turn off your Television now.
Turn off your radio immediately
The Services end. At the same time
Secure explosion plugs in the ears
Of each member of your family. Take
Down your plasma flasks. Give your children
The pills marked one and two
In the C.D. green container, then put
Them to bed. Do not break
The inside airlock seals until
The radiation All Clear shows
(Watch for the cuckoo in your
perspex panel), or your District
Touring Doctor rings your bell.
If before this, your air becomes
Exhausted or if any of your family
Is critically injured, administer
The capsules marked 'Valley Forge'
(Red pocket in No. 1 Survival Kit)

For painless death. (Catholics
Will have been instructed by their priests
What to do in this eventuality.)
This announcement is ending. Our President
Has already given orders for
Massive retaliation—it will be
Decisive. Some of us may die.
Remember, statistically
It is not likely to be you.
All flags are flying fully dressed
On Government buildings—the sun is shining.
Death is the least we have to fear.
We are all in the hands of God,
Whatever happens happens by His Will.
Now go quickly to your shelters.

Peter Porter

BLACKBIRD

Blackbird by pondered phrase
Talks in the eve of dusk,
In pale trembling sun when fails
The north which breathed all day,
And the lamb clouds melt to blue.
Blackbird from wintered elm
Deliberate and calm
Studies each phrase,
Each phrase for a full song.
Tongues of evening fire
Lick the elm top where he sings,
Where he quickens his phrase
And ruffles and arches and swells
And strides a pace on the black bough,
Clear fluting to me below
In the brief cold fiery dusk.

Frank Prewett

TWENTIETH-CENTURY MOTHER

Rocking the cradle of his child
I used to watch the bombers wane,
And wish him peace and wish them well.
For then my heart was reconciled
To bombs, theirs, ours, the heartless rain
On just, unjust. O what the hell!
To stop the killing sooner, I,
We all, must think of ends, not means . . .
(And that became my rock-a-bye)
There could be peace before she weans.

Our child now marches through the town,
Bearing her own child as she goes,
To point the slogan, to protest
Against a threat that no one knows
From faceless men of no renown.
No what-the-hell: no for-the-best.
There are no ends: spare us the means.
There could be war before she weans.

John Pudney

SPIDER

Now, the spires of a privet fork from the hedge
And stretch a web between them;
The spider-nub eases his grip a trifle, twists a thread safe,
And the afternoon is quiet again.

Damp clouds drift above him; a burst of rain
Runs him back along a vane

To a leaf-shed, while it beads his web
And raises weed-smells from below
Of vetch, fumitory, and small mallow.

Hanging there are a dozen or so
Brown shells which tremble.
The curtain is ripped from the sun, and grass again
Leaps into its fumble:

Ants totter with their medicine balls and cabers, stone walls
Pop with their crickets;
A bluefly, furry as a dog, squares up
To the web and takes it with a jump like a hoop

And spider springs round like a man darting
To the fringes of a dogfight;

Tugging like a frantic sailor, buzzing like a jerky sawyer,
Fly finishes in swaddling
Tight as a knot
From the spinnerets' glistening.

And though spider
Hangs a little lower than the sun
Over all their heads, all
Seem ignorant of that passing;
The afternoon, the ebullience increases
Among the low boughs of the weeds
And spider steady, like a lichened glove
Only a little lower than the sun; none
Takes account of that to and fro passing,
Or of the manner of that death in swaddling.

Peter Redgrove

THE TRAVELLERS

Approve the traveller who never went;
Slippers and timetables supply his want.

Admire the traveller who went, and stayed,
Renewing life in some rare latitude.

Honour the traveller who went, and died,
Raised above gain or failure by the deed.

But the returning traveller with a store
Of memoirs and an ancient-mariner stare

Shall be discredited from bar to bar
And in the end account himself a bore.

James Reeves

SPICER'S INSTANT POETRY

On sale everywhere: Spicer's Instant Poetry.
Trial size, 2/–; epic pack, 19/6.
A balanced mixture of clichés, catchwords,
Symbols, non sequiturs, ambiguities,
Stock phrases and borrowings from the best models.
Warranted free from superfluous emotion,
Bad rhymes and obvious plagiarism.
Simply add luke-warm milk and water.
A child can use it.
One teaspoonful reconstitutes a sonnet.
This infallible preparation
Makes poems suitable for competitions,
National and international festivals,

Private greetings cards and autograph albums.
Results guaranteed, and are to be seen
In best literary journals.
Spicer's Instant Poetry comes in seven popular shades:
Nature (including animals), childhood, domestic troubles,
Industry and politics, thwarted love,
Mythology and religion, foreign parts.
Special 'Parnassus' kit containing all the above varieties,
Free surprise item and coloured art portrait of leading bard,
Or 'Tartan Special' for Scottish subjects,
Five shillings only, post free.
Extra strong mix for homosexual or surgical pieces.
Delighted user writes: 'Instant Poetry
Is a joy for ever . . . Indistinguishable from the real thing.'
Order now and astonish your friends.
Big cash opportunities: Immortality
Assured or money returned.

James Reeves

THE PIKE

The river turns,
Leaving a place for the eye to rest,
A furred, a rocky pool,
A bottom of water.

The crabs tilt and eat, leisurely,
And the small fish lie, without shadow, motionless,
Or drift lazily in and out of the weeds.
The bottom-stones shimmer back their irregular striations,
And the half-sunken branch bends away from the gazer's
    eye.

A scene for the self to abjure!—
And I lean, almost into the water,
My eye always beyond the surface reflection;
I lean, and love these manifold shapes,
Until, out from a dark cove,
From beyond the end of a mossy log,
With one sinuous ripple, then a rush,
A thrashing-up of the whole pool,
The pike strikes.

Theodore Roethke

HEARD IN A VIOLENT WARD

In heaven, too,
You'd be institutionalized.
But that's all right,—
If they let you eat and swear
With the likes of Blake,
And Christopher Smart,
And that sweet man, John Clare.

Theodore Roethke

THE GERANIUM

When I put her out, once, by the garbage pail,
She looked so limp and bedraggled,
So foolish and trusting, like a sick poodle,
Or a wizened aster in late September,
I brought her back in again
For a new routine—
Vitamins, water, and whatever

Sustenance seemed sensible
At the time: she'd lived
So long on gin, bobbie pins, half-smoked cigars, dead beer,
Her shrivelled petals falling
On the faded carpet, the stale
Steak grease stuck to her fuzzy leaves.
(Dried-out, she creaked like a tulip.)

The things she endured!—
The dumb dames shrieking half the night
Or the two of us, alone, both seedy,
Me breathing booze at her,
She leaning out of her pot toward the window.

Near the end, she seemed almost to hear me—
And that was scary—
So when that snuffling cretin of a maid
Threw her, pot and all, into the trash-can,
I said nothing.

But I sacked the presumptuous hag the next week,
I was that lonely.

Theodore Roethke

ELEGY

Her face like a rain-beaten stone on the day she rolled off
With the dark hearse, and enough flowers for an
    alderman,—
And so she was, in her way, Aunt Tilly.

Sighs, sighs, who says they have sequence?
Between the spirit and the flesh,—what war?
She never knew;

For she asked no quarter and gave none,
Who sat with the dead when the relatives left,
Who fed and tended the infirm, the mad, the epileptic,
And, with a harsh rasp of a laugh at herself,
Faced up to the worst.

I recall how she harried the children away all the late
    summer
From the one beautiful thing in her yard, the peachtree;
How she kept the wizened, the fallen, the misshapen for
    herself,
And picked and pickled the best, to be left on rickety
    doorsteps.

And yet she died in agony,
Her tongue, at the last, thick, black as an ox's.

Terror of cops, bill collectors, betrayers of the poor,—
I see you in some celestial supermarket,
Moving serenely among the leeks and cabbages,
Probing the squash,
Bearing down, with two steady eyes,
On the quaking butcher.

Theodore Roethke

AUTOSTRADA DEL SOLE

At 660 kms most are left standing—
Fiats, Fords, Volvos, Peugeots.

But occasionally, eye to mirror, a blur is demanding
Attention, a Lancia or Ferrari. You've had your lot.

To the SUN: it claims you, big as an AGIP
Sign, and as efficient. Put your foot down, let it rip.

Overhead, bridges are functional, concrete and cement
Gleaming. A swept landscape, wherever you came from or
    went.

Intoxication of motels, clearways, the colourless blue.
But asphalt seduces, don't pause, just go through.

Those signposts, what do they offer? Piacenza, Parma,
Cremona, Ravenna. Don't let on, it won't harm her

To miss out basilicas and mosaics. Stop
Instead at Bologna, for *pasta*, fill her up,

She'll stop fretting; edge the guide from her lap.
After all, it's the SUN you're chasing, there's no trap.

Haystacks like dolls' houses, vineyards, olives—they're
There all right, out of sight with the peasants. But air,

Think of the air, blue sea, *arragoste* and *scampi*.
Forget her expression, she's playing at being grumpy.

It's the mileage that matters; flick the flies from the wind-
    screen
This is the *mezzogiorno*, your conscience is clean.

Alan Ross

NEAR CARTHAGE

Whiteness so white here it enthralls,
Whiteness of sails and walls,
Sea-salt and soda.

Yet everywhere touched by gold,
Minarets and beaches, the old
Palaces, young skins.

And blue like some lotion
Of heaven on mosque and ocean,
In assassinating eyes.

A conjunction of colours to blind us—
Yet running me through
At every step with reminders
Of hair that was gold, skin white, eyes blue.

Alan Ross

AGEING SCHOOLMASTER

And now another autumn morning finds me
    With chalk dust on my sleeve and in my breath,
Preoccupied with vague, habitual speculation
    On the huge inevitability of death.

Not wholly wretched, yet knowing absolutely
    That I shall never reacquaint myself with joy,
I sniff the smell of ink and chalk and my mortality
    And think of when I rolled, a gormless boy,

And rollicked round the playground of my hours,
    And wonder when precisely tolled the bell
Which summoned me from summer liberties
    And brought me to this chill autumnal cell

From which I gaze upon the april faces
    That gleam before me, like apples ranged on shelves,
And yet I feel no pinch or prick of envy
    Nor would I have them know their sentenced selves.

With careful effort I can separate the faces,
    The dull, the clever, the various shapes and sizes,
But in the autumn shades I find I only
    Brood upon death, who carries off all the prizes.

Vernon Scannell

AUTOBIOGRAPHICAL NOTE

Beeston, the place, near Nottingham:
We lived there for three years or so.
Each Saturday at two-o'clock
We queued up for the matinée,
All the kids for streets around
With snotty noses, giant caps,
Cut down coats and heavy boots,
The natural enemies of cops
And schoolteachers. Profane and hoarse
We scrambled, yelled and fought until
The Picture Palace opened up
And we, like Hamelin children, forced
Our bony way into the hall.
That much is easy to recall;
Also the reek of chewing-gum,
Gob-stoppers and liquorice,
But of the flickering myths themselves
Not much remains. The hero was
A milky wide-brimmed hat, a shape
Astride the arched white stallion;
The villain's horse and hat were black.
Disbelief did not exist
And laundered virtue always won
With quicker gun and harder fist,
And all of us applauded it.
Yet I remember moments when
In solitude I'd find myself

Brooding on the sooty man,
The bristling villain, who could move
Imagination in a way
The well-shaved hero never could,
And even warm the nervous heart
With something oddly close to love.

Vernon Scannell

REMEMBRANCE DAY

Apposite blood red the blobs
Of artificial poppies count
Our annual dead.
The garment of lament is worn
Threadbare and each medal hangs
Heavy its shameful head.

Bugles make their sad assault
Upon the heart and spine and throat
Ordering regret.
The names evoked are usual:
Passchendaele, Bapaume and Loos—
Our cheeks are wet.

And fumbling for the right response
We summon names more personal:
Nobby, Frank and Ted.
But wormy years have eaten their
Identities and none can mourn
These artificial dead.

And when a true emotion strikes
It strikes a crude, unsanctioned blow
Which brings a harsher chill
To hearts that know that they grow old
And must grow older yet before
That terrible Until.

Vernon Scannell

WALKING WOUNDED

A mammoth morning moved grey flanks and groaned.
In the rusty hedges pale rags of mist hung;
The gruel of mud and leaves in the mauled lane
Smelled sweet, like blood. Birds had died or flown,
Their green and silent attics sprouting now
With branches of leafed steel, hiding round eyes
And ripe grenades ready to drop and burst.
In the ditch at the cross-roads the fallen rider lay
Hugging his dead machine and did not stir
At crunch of mortar, tantrum of a Bren
Answering a Spandau's manic jabber.
Then into sight the ambulance came,
Stumbling and churning past the broken farm,
The amputated sign-post and smashed trees,
Slow wagonloads of bandaged cries, square trucks
That rolled on ominous wheels, vehicles
Made mythopoeic by their mortal freight
And crimson crosses on the dirty white.
This grave procession passed, though, for a while,
The grinding of their engines could be heard,
A dark noise on the pallor of the morning,
Dark as dried blood; and then it faded, died.
The road was empty, but it seemed to wait—
Like a stage which knows the cast is in the wings—
Wait for a different traffic to appear.
The mist still hung in snags from dripping thorns;
Absent-minded guns still sighed and thumped.
And then they came, the walking wounded,
Straggling the road like convicts loosely chained,
Dragging at ankles exhaustion and despair.
Their heads were weighted down by last night's lead,
And eyes still drank the dark. They trailed the night
Along the morning road. Some limped on sticks;
Others wore rough dressings, splints and slings;
A few had turbanned heads, the dirty cloth

Brown-badged with blood. A humble brotherhood,
Not one was suffering from a lethal hurt,
They were not magnified by noble wounds,
There was no splendour in that company.
And yet, remembering after eighteen years,
In the heart's throat a sour sadness stirs;
Imagination pauses and returns
To see them walking still, but multiplied
In thousands now. And when heroic corpses
Turn slowly in their decorated sleep
And every ambulance has disappeared
The walking wounded still trudge down that lane,
And when recalled they must bear arms again.

Vernon Scannell

THE GREAT WAR

Whenever war is spoken of
I find
The war that was called Great invades the mind:
The grey militia marches over land
A darker mood of grey
Where fractured tree-trunks stand
And shells, exploding, open sudden fans
Of smoke and earth.
Blind murders scythe
The deathscape where the iron brambles writhe;
The sky at night
Is honoured with rosettes of fire,
Flares that define the corpses on the wire
As terror ticks on wrists at zero hour.
These things I see,
But they are only part
Of what it is that slyly probes the heart:
Less vivid images and words excite

The sensuous memory
And, even as I write,
Fear and a kind of love collaborate
To call each simple conscript up
For quick inspection:
Trenches' parapets
Paunchy with sandbags; bandoliers, tin-hats,
Candles in dug-outs,
Duckboards, mud and rats.
Then, like patrols, tunes creep into the mind:
A long, long trail, The Rose of No-Man's-Land,
Home Fires and *Tipperary;*
And through the misty keening of a band
Of Scottish pipes the proper names are heard
Like fateful commentary of distant guns:
Passchendaele, Bapaume, and Loos, and Mons.
And now,
Whenever the November sky
Quivers with a bugle's hoarse, sweet cry,
The reason darkens; in its evening gleam
Crosses and flares, tormented wire, grey earth
Splattered with crimson flowers,
And I remember,
Not the war I fought in
But the one called Great
Which ended in a sepia November
Four years before my birth.

Vernon Scannell

THE MEN WHO WEAR MY CLOTHES

Sleepless I lay last night and watched the slow
    Procession of the men who wear my clothes:
First, the grey man with bloodshot eyes and sly
    Gestures miming what he loves and loathes.

Next came the cheery knocker-back of pints,
    The beery joker, never far from tears,
Whose loud and public vanity acquaints
    The careful watcher with his private fears.

And then I saw the neat-mouthed gentle man
    Defer politely, listen to the lies,
Smile at the tedious tale and gaze upon
    The little mirrors in the speaker's eyes.

The men who wear my clothes walked past my bed
    And all of them looked tired and rather old;
I felt a chip of ice melt in my blood.
    Naked I lay last night, and very cold.

Vernon Scannell

AUTUMN

It is the football season once more
And the back pages of the Sunday papers
Again show the blurred anguish of goalkeepers.

In Maida Vale, Golders Green and Hampstead
Lamps ripen early in the surprising dusk;
They are furred like stale rinds with a fuzz of mist.

The pavements of Kensington are greasy;
The wind smells of burnt porridge in Bayswater,
And the leaves are mushed to silence in the gutter.

The big hotel like an anchored liner
Rides near the park; lit windows hammer the sky.
Like the slow swish of surf the tyres of taxis sigh.

On Ealing Broadway the cinema glows
Warm behind glass while mellow the church clock chimes
As the waiting girls stir in their delicate chains.

Their eyes are polished by the wind,
But the gleam is dumb, empty of joy or anger.
Though the lovers are long in coming the girls still linger.

We are nearing the end of the year.
Under the sombre sleeve the blood ticks faster
And in the dark ear of Autumn quick voices whisper.

It is a time of year that's to my taste,
Full of spiced rumours, sharp and velutinous flavours,
Dim with the mist that softens the cruel surfaces,
Makes mirrors vague. It is the mist that I most favour.

Vernon Scannell

RUMINANT

The leather belly shades the buttercups.
Her horns are the yellow of old piano keys.
Hopelessly the tail flicks at the humming heat;
Flies crawl to the pools of her eyes.
She slowly turns her head and watches me
As I approach; her gaze is a silent moo.
I stop and we swap stares. I smoke. She chews.

How do I view her then? As pastoral furniture,
Solid in the green and fluid summer?
A brooding factory of milk and sausages,
Or something to be chopped to bits and sold
In wounded paper parcels? No, as none of these.
My view is otherwise and infantile,

But it survives my own sour sneers.
It is the anthropomorphic fallacy
Which puts brown speculation in those eyes.
But I am taken in: that gentleness endears,
As does the massive patience and submission
Huge among buttercups and flies.
But, in the end, it is those plushy eyes,
The slow and meditative jaws, that hold
Me to this most untenable of views:
Almost, it seems, she might be contemplating
Composing a long poem about Ted Hughes.

Vernon Scannell

STRATEGY

Wiser, no doubt, to think of war in terms
of shaded maps, observing with what ease
the black and strictly impersonal line ploughs
deeply, reaping a harvest of towns—the names,

if tongue can sheave them, yours to string upon
the day's objective talk; safer to count
the score in planes, without extravagant
recourse to actual costs in minds or men.

Yet, for all your fables, you cannot avert
the untenable moment of knowing. Tidy
on wind and spiralling height, the falcon already
prepares its tearing descent to your heart.

Since every combatant's wound is your wound, too;
for every death, life pins the crime on you.

Howard Sergeant

A CURSE AGAINST ELEGIES

Oh, love, why do we argue like this?
I am tired of all your pious talk.
Also, I am tired of all the dead.
They refuse to listen,
so leave them alone.
Take your foot out of the graveyard,
they are busy being dead.

Everyone was always to blame:
the last empty fifth of booze,
the rusty nails and chicken feathers
that stuck in the mud on the back doorstep,
the worms that lived under the cat's ear
and the thin-lipped preacher
who refused to call
except once on a flea-ridden day
when he came scuffing in through the yard
looking for a scapegoat.
I hid in the kitchen under the ragbag.

I refuse to remember the dead.
And the dead are bored with the whole thing.
But you—you go ahead,
go on, go on back down
into the graveyard,
lie down where you think their faces are;
talk back to your old bad dreams.

Anne Sexton

LULLABY

It is a summer evening.
The yellow moths sag
against the locked screens

and the faded curtains
suck over the window sills
and from another building
a goat calls in his dreams.
This is the TV parlour
in the best ward at Bedlam.
The night nurse is passing
out the evening pills.
She walks on two erasers,
padding by us one by one.

My sleeping pill is white.
It is a splendid pearl;
it floats me out of myself,
my stung skin as alien
as a loose bolt of cloth.
I will ignore the bed.
I am linen on a shelf.
Let the others moan in secret;
let each lost butterfly
go home. Old woollen head,
take me like a yellow moth
while the goat calls hush-
a-bye.

Anne Sexton

RINGING THE BELLS

And this is the way they ring
the bells in Bedlam
and this is the bell-lady
who comes each Tuesday morning
to give us a music lesson
and because the attendants make you go

and because we mind by instinct,
like bees caught in the wrong hive,
we are the circle of the crazy ladies
who sit in the lounge of the mental house
and smile at the smiling woman
who passes us each a bell,
who points at my hand
that holds my bell, E flat,
and this is the grey dress next to me
who grumbles as if it were special
to be old, to be old,
and this is the small hunched squirrel girl
on the other side of me
who picks at the hairs over her lip,
who picks at the hairs over her lip all day,
and this is how the bells really sound,
as untroubled and clean
as a workable kitchen,
and this is always my bell responding
to my hand that responds to the lady
who points at me, E flat;
and although we are no better for it,
they tell you to go. And you do.

Anne Sexton

WOODS

Woods are for looking at from a distance
On your father's arms;
Woods are for being frightened of—
Bogie-men swing and chunter in those close-packed trees.

Woods are then for making fires in
Running before the wrath of cop or farmer;
Smoke and the smell of dandelions
In place of blood.

Later for loving girls in
Untidy bushes lick damp air
Secret, dark and out of sight
With nothing now to replace blood.

Some use woods for attacking and defending
The black scream of unnatural possession
Tree roots linchpinned into earth
By shudders and the soil of death.

By summer shunned in fear of lightning
The bitter roaming flash of snaked lightning.
In winter shelter us from rain or snow.
Tree-packs hold our fate like cards.

Woods are then forgotten two-score years
Power lapsing into midnight dreams
The core of body and soul
Scooped out by the knife of living.

The wood became jungle, and you its shadow
Woods a purple rage of wakened dogs
To be kept out of, snubbed
Hemmed into night, not known.

Woods returned, tamed, not now for
Making love or fires in.
Familiar; suspicious of their shelter
You stay at home in rain or snow—

The woods are seen but not remembered
A far-off shadow, cloud or dream;
Your power vanishes with theirs—
No more to be defended, or attacked.

Alan Sillitoe

POEM WRITTEN IN MAJORCA

Not here, not here in these clear skies
Where olives in December shed their milk
Has Death power;
Here contentment does not rape and slay
For the mere scent of agony,
But plays with its progenitor the sun
That at each day's beginning spreads
A supine warmth upon the mountain.

Death you need not fear on this island,
Too far south and temperate
To undermine and strike,
Whose agents in this mid-land sea
(Of olive and ghost and silver moon
Full upon a midnight crest),
For nothing count;
Not edge of black nor weight of blade enough
Has Death to thrust-and-drag its angel wings
By Hades' open doors.

But on that other island, where hemlock stones
Stand at the foot of cold Druidic hills,
Death has power.
There I was born, when deep snow lay
Beneath bare willow trees, and groaning frost
Boomed along grey ponds at afternoon,
Frightening birds that,
Though hardened for long winters,
Fled from the nerve-filled ground
And beat their soundless wings away
From Death's first inflicted wound.

Alan Sillitoe

CARTHAGE

Scorpions lurk under loose stones
Marked on Leipzig maps, and electric tramways
Ride shallow loops over thrown-up bones;
Eternal dust guides shadowed gangways

To Punic necropolia tombed-out
In timeless tangents, watched by upstart towers
Of a young cathedral, basilicas combed-out
By time's long competition and the hours

Of each's ruin. The shadow of Christ
And Hamilcar and the later dead
Back up the ancient argument: that whims are diced
Out by the timeless laugh of heaven. The bled

Lips of this crumbling village, with the begging cry
Of children, prove that stone and scorpion lie.

Alan Sillitoe

AMERICAN POETRY

Whatever it is, it must have
A stomach that can digest
Rubber, coal, uranium, moons, poems.

Like the shark, it contains a shoe.
It must swim for miles through the desert
Uttering cries that are almost human.

Louis Simpson

FROGS

The storm broke, and it rained,
And water rose in the pool,
And frogs hopped into the gutter,

With their skins of yellow and green,
And just their eyes shining above the surface
Of the warm solution of slime.

At night, when fireflies trace
Light-lines between the trees and flowers
Exhaling perfume,

The frogs speak to each other
In rhythm. The sound is monstrous,
But their voices are filled with satisfaction.

In the city I pine for the country;
In the country I long for conversation—
Our happy croaking.

Louis Simpson

THE REDWOODS

Mountains are moving, rivers
are hurrying. But we
are still.

We have the thoughts of giants—
clouds, and at night the stars.

And we have names—guttural, grotesque—
Hamet, Og—names with no syllables.

And perish, one by one, our roots
gnawed by the mice. And fall.

And are too slow for death, and change
to stone. Or else too quick,

like candles in a fire. Giants
are lonely. We have waited long

for someone. By our waiting, surely
there must be someone at whose touch

our boughs would bend; and hands
to gather us; a spirit

to whom we are light as the hawthorn tree.
O if there is a poet

let him come now! We stand at the Pacific
like great unmarried girls,

turning in our heads the stars and clouds,
considering whom to please.

Louis Simpson

THE WAR ORPHANS

*(Written after seeing a photograph of Korean children
asleep in the snow)*

The snow is the blood of these poor Dead ... they have
   no other—
These children, old in the dog's scale of years, too old
For the hopeless breast—ghosts for whom there is none
   to care,

Grown fleshless as the skeleton
Of Adam, they have known
More aeons of the cold than he endured
In the first grave of the world. They have, for bed,
The paving stones, the spider spins their blankets, and
  their bread
Is the shred and crumb of dead Chance. In this epoch of
  the cold,
In which new worlds are formed, new glaciations
To overcast the world that was the heart,
There is only that architecture of the winter, the huge plan
Of the lasting skeleton, built from the hunger of Man,
Constructed for hunger—piteous in its griefs, the
  humiliation
Of outworn flesh, the Ape-cerement, O the foolish
  tattered clothing,
Rags stained with the filth of humanity, stink of its toiling,
But never the smell of the heart, with its warmth, its
  fevers,
Rapacity and grandeur. For the cold is zero
In infinite intensity, brother to democratic
Death, our one equality, who holds
Alike the maelstrom of the blood, the world's incendiarism,
The summer redness and the hope of the rose,
The beast, and man's superiority o'er the beast
That is but this:
Man bites with his smile, and poisons with his kiss.
When, in each dawn,
The light on my brow is changed to the mark of Cain,
And my blood cries 'Am I my brother's keeper?' seeing
  these ghosts
Of Man's forgetfulness of Man, I feel again
The pitiless but healing rain—who thought I only
Had the lonely Lethe flood for tears.

Edith Sitwell

WEST PENWITH

These are the people of exodus.
Badger, seal, and gull
watch the dark faces and stiff hands
answer the journeying call.

Bells in the hollow cages
swing to the tide of night;
hymns from the granite chapels
drift through the emptied streets.

These are from Egypt, travelling
the bleak of the wide moor;
the badger's holt has tunnelled
under the histories floor.

Stones in their moonshine circles
stare at the crossing hand;
shells of the tall mine buildings
shake at the west wind.

Silent and empty handed
the leader comes from Chun;
the seal's voice lifts across the stones
her undefeated tune.

Carns in their lonely ghosting
answer no one's hope;
over the harbour deep the gull
screams like a running rope.

These are the people of exodus;
moor and wave and wind
crowd round the white and squatting farms
and the west walls are blind.

Robin Skelton

RYTHM

They dunno how it is. I smack a ball
right through the goals. But they dunno how the words
get muddled in my head, get tired somehow.
I look through the window, see. And there's a wall
I'd kick the ball against, just smack and smack.
Old Jerry he can't play, he don't know how,
not now at any rate. He's too flicking small.
See him in shorts, out in the crazy black.
Rythm, he says, and ryme. See him at back.
He don't know nuthing about Law. He'd fall
flat on his face, just like a big sack,
when you're going down the wing, the wind behind you
and crossing into the goalmouth and they're roaring
the whole great crowd. They're up on their feet cheering.
The ball's at your feet and there it goes, just crack.
Old Jerry dives—the wrong way. And they're jearing
and I run to the centre and old Bash
jumps up and down, and I feel great, and wearing
my gold and purpel strip, fresh from the wash.

Iain Crichton Smith

AT THE HIGHLAND GAMES

Like re-reading a book which has lost its pith.

Watching the piper dandying over a sodden stage
saluting an empty tent.

The empty beer glasses catch the sun
sparkle like old brooches against green.

Fur-hatted, with his huge twirling silver stick
the pipe-major has gypsy cheekbones, colour of brick.

Everything drowses. The stewards with aloof eagle stare
sit on collapsing rock, chair on brown chair.

Once the pibroch showed the grave 'ground'
of seas without bubbles, where great hulks were drowned,

meat with moustaches. The heroic dead die
over and over the sea to misty Skye.

Past the phantom ivy, bird song, I walk
among crew-cuts, cameras, the heather-covered rock,

past my ancestry, peasant, men who bowed
with stony necks to the daughter-stealing lord.

Past my ancestry, the old songs, the pibroch
stirring my consciousness like the breeze a loch

Past my buried heart my friend who complains
of 'All the crime, their insane violence'.

Stone by stone the castles crumble. The seas
have stored away their great elegies.

'Morag of Dunvegan.' Dandy piper
with delicate soft paws, knee-bending stepper,

saluting an empty tent. Blue-kilted stewards
strut like strange storks along the sodden sward.

Finished. All of it's finished. The Gaelic
boils in my mouth, the South Sea silver stick

twirls, settles. The mannequins are here.
Calum, how you'd talk of their glassy stare,

their loud public voices. Stained pictures
of what was raw, violent, alive and coarse.

I watch their heirs, Caligulas with canes
stalk in their rainbow kilts towards the dance.

Iain Crichton Smith

BOTH HARVESTS

Guns twitch the gloved ears of the rabbit,
that ripened with the corn. Summer
was burrowed, with the young peering
over green shoots. Now they move
under red corn. But blades are set
and honed. A tractor roves the scythed
edges. These men who stook and bend,
bend and stook, have their business
with grain. Those who come after,
come to kill, gun under shoulder.
A rabbit is a grey thing running,
stopped, hung in air, dead. Some
hide under bound sheaves. Some panic
into the mower and are savaged, blood,
bone, and pelt. Set blades are determined.
Rabbits die running, not like standing grain
cut clean. The field is clear, its straw
lined and ordered: it will be bread
and bedding for safe cattle. The rabbit
need not fear the winter. Shot corpses
brace under fur, are shared out evenly.

Ken Smith

BOG-FACE

Dear little Bog-Face,
Why are you so cold?
And why do you lie with your eyes shut?—
You are not very old.

I am a Child of this World,
And a Child of Grace,
And Mother, I shall be glad when it is over,
I am Bog-Face.

Stevie Smith

AT SCHOOL

*(A Paolo and Francesca situation but more hopeful,
say in Purgatory)*

At school I always walk with Elwyn
Walk with Elwyn all the day
Oh my darling darling Elwyn
We shall never go away.

This school is a most curious place
Everything happens faintly
And the other boys and girls who are here
We cannot see distinctly.

All the day I walk with Elwyn
And sometimes we also ride
Both of us would always really
Rather be outside.

Most I like to ride with Elwyn
In the early morning sky
Under the solitary mosses
That hang from the trees awry.

*The wind blows cold then
And the wind comes to the dawn
And we ride silently
And kiss as we ride down.*

Oh my darling darling Elwyn
Oh what a sloppy love is ours
Oh how this sloppy love sustains us
When we get back to the school bars.

There are bars round this school
And inside the lights are always burning bright
And yet there are shadows
That belong rather to the night than to the light.

Oh my darling darling Elwyn
Why is there this dusty heat in this closed school?
All the radiators must be turned full on
Surely that is against the rules?

Hold my hand as we run down the long corridors
Arched over with tombs
We are underground now a long way
Look out, we are getting close to the boiler room.

We are not driven harshly to the lessons you know
That go on under the electric lights
That go on persistently, patiently you might say,
They do not mind if we are not very bright.

Open this door quick, Elwyn, it is break-time
And if we ride quickly we can come to the sea-pool
And swim; will not that be a nice thing to do?
Oh my darling do not look so sorrowful.

Oh why do we cry so much
Why do we not go to some place that is nice?
Why do we only stand close
And lick the tears from each other's eyes?

Darling, my darling
You are with me in the school and in the dead trees' glade
If you were not with me
I should be afraid.

Fear not the ragged dawn skies
Fear not the heat of the boiler room
Fear not the sky where it flies
The jagged clouds in their rusty colour.

Do not tell me not to cry my love
The tears run down your face too
There is still half an hour left
Can we not think of something to do?

There goes the beastly bell
Tolling us to lessons
If I do not like this place much
That bell is the chief reason.

Oh darling Elwyn love
Our tears fall down together
It is because of the place we're in
And because of the weather.

Stevie Smith

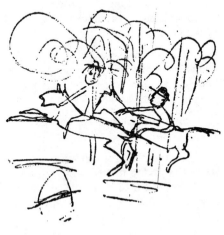

THE GRANGE

Oh there hasn't been much change
At the Grange,

Of course the blackberries growing closer
Make getting in a bit of a poser,
But there hasn't been much change
At the Grange.

Old Sir Prior died,
They say on the point of leaving for the seaside,
They never found the body, which seemed odd to some
(Not me, seeing as what I seen the butler done.)

Oh there hasn't been much change
At the Grange.

The governess 'as got it now,
Miss Ursy 'aving moved down to the Green Cow—
Proper done out of 'er rights, she was, a b. shame.
And what's that the governess pushes round at nights in the
    old pram?

Oh there hasn't been much change
At the Grange.

The shops leave supplies at the gate now, meat, groceries,
Mostly old tinned stuff you know from McInnes's,
They wouldn't go up to the door,
Not after what happened to Fred's pa.

Oh there hasn't been much change
At the Grange.

Parssing there early this morning, cor lummy,
I 'ears a whistling sound coming from the old chimney,
Whistling it was fit to bust and not a note wrong,
The old pot, whistling The Death of Nelson.

No there hasn't been much change
At the Grange,

But few goes that way somehow,
Not now.

Stevie Smith

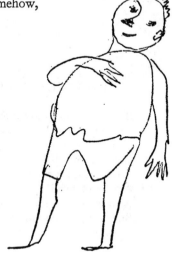

A SUNDAY

A black Cordoba hat tilted
and the chin-strap
make it.

And she his white mare
with tail coiffured
coming in dancing
(her eyes of a tragedienne)
speak it.

Crowd-din like gravel falling;
an odour of expectation
and that odour

Which rounds her fastidious nostrils:
blood sweetening the air
of evening and October.

Bernard Spencer

SHALL THESE BONES LIVE?

If all the clocks rang their last chime,
And all the clock-towers toppled, and time
Ran down today,
Chaucer and Blake's haphazard bones
Would not lift their Abbey stones;
And stalk away
Arm in arm, to see the sun
Burn out, or the moon's skeleton
Wasting and frail as they.

Dying, they put the body down
Once and for all like an old gown
In its wooden room.
Each has climbed to a worthier nook
Between the white walls of a book
Till the knock of doom.
This secret every poet knows:
His nib must cut with chisel-blows
The lettering of his tomb.

Jon Stallworthy

ROMANCE

Why, when my head was filled
With maidens for whose sake
Kings sold their castles, headsmen felled
A forest of tall princes, and
The woodcutter's sons were drowned in the lake;

Why, when my heroines
Sang Te Deums from the rack;
From faggots rampant at their shins;
Or, tossed between sea and sand,
Elbowed the lighthouse dinghy to the wreck;

Why should I look, not once,
But ever since, answer me that,
At you with no falcon nor lance
But a basket in your hand,
And, for a crown, your least heraldic hat?

Jon Stallworthy

FIRST BLOOD

It was. The breach smelling of oil,
The stock of resin—buried snug
In the shoulder. Not too much recoil
At the firing of the first slug

(Jubilantly into the air)
Nor yet too little. Targets pinned
Against a tree: shot down: and there
Abandoned to the sniping wind.

My turn first to carry the gun.
Indian file and camouflaged
With contours of green shade and sun
We ghosted between larch and larch.

A movement between branches—thump
Of a fallen cone. The barrel
Jumps, making branches jump
Higher, dislodging the squirrel

To the next tree. Your turn, my turn.
The silhouette retracts its head.
A hit. 'Let's go back to the lawn.'
'We can't leave it carrying lead

For the rest of its life. Reload.
Finish him off. Reload again.'
It was now *him*, and when he showed
The sky cracked like a window pane.

He broke away: traversed a full
Half dozen trees: vanished. Had found
A hole? We watched that terrible
Slow spiral to the clubbing ground.

His back was to the tree. His eyes
Were gun barrels. He was dumb,
And we could not see past the size
Of his hands or hear for the drum

In his side. Four shots point-blank
To dull his eyes, a fifth to stop
The shiver in his clotted flank.
A fling of earth. As we stood up

The larches closed their ranks. And when
Earth would not muffle the drumming blood
We, like dishonoured soldiers, ran
The gauntlet of a darkening wood.

Jon Stallworthy

THEN

Then every snowfall was a new beginning,
A natural frontier in time to be
Crossed as never before, breathlessly.
Christmas Eve, New Year's Eve and the going back
To school flickered like milestones, but white leaves
   spinning
From besom trees stopped time dead in our tracks.

The books were balanced overnight: credit
And debit columns cancelled themselves out,
And the new account opened with a shout
For Wellington boots. Finding that clean sheet
Smooth to the walls of the house, what profit
Figures followed our toboggans and feet!

Still the new leaf turns over, but we know
The books will not balance today: we must
Carry ambition over, loss and lust.
Years overlap, have no clean start or end.
Faced by the superb innocence of snow,
Still, for an hour or two, we can pretend.

Jon Stallworthy

'HERE COMES SIR GEORGE'

The boys wink at the boys: 'Here comes Sir George.'
Yes, here he comes, punctual as nine o'clock
With bad jokes buzzing at his ramrod back—
'Victoria's Uncle', 'Rearguard of the Raj'.

They do not know or, if they know, forget
The old fool held a province down larger
Than England; not as a Maharaja
Prodigal with silver and bayonet;

But with cool sense, authority and charm
That still attend him, crossing a room
With the *Odes of Horace* under his arm
And in his button-hole a fresh-cut bloom.

Honour the rearguard, you half-men: for it
Was, in retreat, the post of honour. He—
Last of the titans—is worth your study.
You are not worth the unsheathing of his wit.

Jon Stallworthy

NO ORDINARY SUNDAY

No ordinary Sunday. First the light
Falling dead through dormitory windows blind
With fog; and then, at breakfast, every plate
Stained with the small, red cotton flower; and no
Sixpence for pocketmoney. Greatcoats, lined
By the right, marched from their pegs, with slow
Poppy fires smouldering in one lapel
To light us through the fallen cloud. Behind
That handkerchief sobbed the quick Sunday bell.

A granite cross, the school field underfoot,
Inaudible prayers, hymn-sheets that stirred
Too loudly in the hand. When hymns ran out,
Silence, like silt, lay round so wide and deep
It seemed that winter held its breath. We heard
Only the river talking in its sleep:
Until the bugler flexed his lips, and sound
Cutting the fog cleanly like a bird,
Circled and sang out over the bandaged ground.

Then, low voiced, the headmaster called the roll
Of those who could not answer; every name
Suffixed with honour—'double first', 'kept goal
For Cambridge'— and a death—in spitfires, tanks,
And ships torpedoed. At his call there came
Through the mist blond heroes in broad ranks
With rainbows struggling on their chests. Ahead
Of us, in strict step, as we idled home
Marched the formations of the towering dead.

November again, and the bugles blown
In a tropical Holy Trinity,
The heroes today stand further off, grown
Smaller but distinct. They flash no medals, keep
No ranks: through *Last Post* and *Reveille*

Their chins loll on their chests, like birds asleep.
Only when the long, last note ascends
Upon the wings of kites, some two or three
Look up: and have the faces of my friends.

Jon Stallworthy

CAMEL

Though come down in the world to pulling a cart
Piled high as a house-top, camel, your gait
Proclaims, proclaims, proclaims the aristocrat.

Though your knees, like a clown's, wear bells that clash
Whenever your cushion-feet cuff the street,
A greater clown behind you swings the lash

Over your backside. History and he
Are unacquainted. From your ancestors
You have inherited history:

Philosophy becomes you like your hump:
Nobility speaks louder than these sores
And bells and the sweat on your angular rump.

I have seen your nostrils flare to a wind
Born nowhere in the port or festering slums,
But in the wastes beyond the wastes of Sind.

Heavily falls the lash. You neither turn
Nor flinch, but hooded in your eye there comes
A glint of snows above Baluchistan.

Jon Stallworthy

TOWN AND COUNTRY

People who live in towns
Often talk to themselves.
They have little sunlight,
Less quiet, and nothing very fresh to eat.
Loving is quite a problem.

Their pleasures are not all that pleasant,
Though they pay dearly for them.
In a dry summer,
Towns smell of money going bad.

Country people have skins like fruit, and vote like grandad.
They treat cattle like cows,
And speak kindly to strangers—
Though they use too many poisons
Which they buy from towns.

Suburban people are different from either,
Bringing up their gardens.
They are kind by committee,
And smile behind gates.
They are not seen talking to themselves.

Town people try very hard
Not to be taken in.
Sometimes they die of not being taken in
Anywhere by anyone.

The sky grows closer,
The landlords more so.
Chimneys get cleaner,
Green belts blacker.

Gordon Symes

IN CANTERBURY CATHEDRAL

Trees, but straighter than birches, rise to the sky
Of stone. Their branches meet in the sky of stone.
Stone fountains leap and meet: their traceries are
As light as lace. These prayers of stone were prayed
To a God I can't believe in, but were made
By Man, men almost gods, in whom I can
Believe: were made as strong, to last as long
As time. I stare and pray to Man alone.

A. S. J. Tessimond

HEAVEN

In the heaven of the god I hope for (call him X)
There is marriage and giving in marriage and transient sex
For those who will cast the body's vest aside
Soon, but are not yet wholly rarefied
And still embrace. For X is never annoyed
Or shocked; has read his Jung and knows his Freud.
He gives you time in heaven to do as you please,
To climb love's gradual ladder by slow degrees,
Gently to rise from sense to soul, to ascend
To a world of timeless joys, world without end.

Here on the gates of pearl there hangs no sign
Limiting cakes and ale, forbidding wine.
No weakness here is hidden, no vice unknown.
Sin is a sickness to be cured, outgrown
With the help of a god who can laugh, an unsolemn god
Who smiles at old wives' tales of iron rod
And fiery hell, a god who's more at ease
With bawds and Falstaffs than with pharisees.

Here the lame learn to leap, the blind to see.
Tyrants are taught to be humble, slaves to be free.
Fools become wise and wise men cease to be bores.
Here bishops learn from lips of back-street whores,
And white men follow black-faced angels' feet
Through fields of orient and immortal wheat.

A. S. J. Tessimond

LIMBO

The air-gauge clamped our heartbeats. When we searched
the cabin—firm again, relentless—a
stir of limbs confirmed the needle's lurch.
How full of charm proved our young stowaway!

How to tell someone that his offence is mortal
merely in that the fuel his weight would cost, the air
he breathes, is more than one frail cosmic-ship can spare?
His grin said, *Company!* could not believe the portal

that leads to new worlds from this fetid womb
must suck him forth to —limbo. Yet he went
quietly into the airlock. There's no room
for sentiment in space. We meant

him well enough ... Zoë, it's not our fault; you must
eat. We bear supplies for the living, put them first.

D. M. Thomas

LIZARD

Here, where the hooves of the mule cough dust,
In a noon-pulse of the upright sun,
Idles the coiled beat and jet
In slick, esurient lizard's tongue.

Rough-mottled stones in white and grey
Scallop the sharp, volcanic rock
With cone and shelf. The flat tongue sets
Air throbbing with its tiny shock.

Crevice, crevasse, the insect alleys
Channel his thought. In twilight gates
And tracks of lava fissure,
Crepuscular, the lizard waits.

Running the bed of rock's defile
Draws him, predestined, from the day
Of mule and goat-bell; from the stunted
Olives, sloping green to grey.

Cool as a silk, the lithe tongue leaps
Taut at its stretch to drop a fly
Dead as a stone and shelve him deep;
While, like a bomb, the mid-day above
Stuns the white houses into sleep.

Donald Thomas

TANGIER: HOTEL RIF

Pale pink and green lights flush on white
Façades and balconies. All questions are
Steps on dead carpets here: the high-stooled blonde
Imposes on a chromium bar.

As carp in an abandoned pool,
Her slow thoughts turn; through olive waves
Their golden snouts distil the light
In images of deep sky's architraves.

As light from the emerald glass she holds,
Her morning images run waste:
Tired fashions of the mind commend
The wide-paved avenues of taste.

Faint winds fall in a hiss upon
Plumes of the palms: the brown wind stirs
Neat cypress by the hillside tombs,
White marble promenade of fears.

At sand's white rim, on cobalt wave's
Trim verge, sky in slack water blends
With shifting effluence of decay,
Takings and leavings of the sense.

Shells, amber weed, a late tide's scum
Like habit's shrivelled flotsam ride:
No needle fine enough to etch
Such deliquescence of the mind.

Beyond the sun's striped awnings
And coloured bulbs in slack festoons,
Hull-down the bilge-sprung tankers limp
To pale Atlantic afternoons.

Donald Thomas

AFFORESTATION

It's a population of trees
Colonizing the old
Haunts of men; I prefer,
Listening to their talk,

The bare language of grass
To what the woods say,
Standing in black crowds
Under the stars at night
Or in the sun's way.
The grass feeds the sheep;
The sheep give the wool
For warm clothing, but these—?
I see the cheap times
Against which they grow:
Thin houses for dupes,
Pages of pale trash,
A world that has gone sour
With spruce. Cut them down,
They won't take the weight
Of any of the strong bodies
For which the wind sighs.

R. S. Thomas

A COUNTRY

At fifty he was still trying to deceive
Himself. He went out at night,
Imagining the dark country
Between the border and the coast
Was still Wales; the old language
Came to him on the wind's lips;
There were intimations of farms
Whose calendar was a green hill.

And yet under such skies the land
Had no more right to its name
Than a corpse had; self-given wounds
Wasted it. It lay like a bone
Thrown aside and of no use
For anything except shame to gnaw.

R. S. Thomas

TRUTH

He was in the fields, when I set out.
He was in the fields, when I came back.
In between, what long hours,
What centuries might have elapsed.
Did he look up? His arm half
Lifted was more to ward off
My foolishness. You will return,
He intimated; the heart's roots
Are here under this black soil
I labour at. A change of wind
Can bring the smooth town to a stop;
The grass whispers beneath the flags;
Every right word on your tongue
Has a green taste. It is the mind
Calling you, eager to paint
Its distances; but the truth's here,
Closer than the world will confess,
In this bare bone of life that I pick.

R. S. Thomas

HIRELING

Cars pass him by; he'll never own one.
Men won't believe in him for this.
Let them come into the hills
And meet him wandering a road,
Fenced with rain, as I have now;
The wind feathering his hair;
The sky's ruins, gutted with fire
Of the late sun, smouldering still.

Nothing is his, neither the land
Nor the land's flocks. Hired to live
On hills too lonely, sharing his hearth
With cats and hens, he has lost all
Property but the grey ice
Of a face splintered by life's stone.

R. S. Thomas

PORTRAIT

You never asked what he was like,
That man, Prytherch. Did you class him
With other labourers, breaking the wild
Mare of the soil with bare knuckles
And gnarled thighs, knowing him shut
In cold arenas between hedges
With no audience, a man for whom
The stars' bridle was hung too high?

He was in rags; you were right there.
But the blood was fanned by the sharp draught
Of winter into a huge blaze
In the cheeks' grate, and eyes that you might
Have fancied brown from their long gazing
Downward were of a hard blue,
So shrill they would not permit the ear
To hear what the lips' slobber intended.

R. S. Thomas

FOR THE RECORD

What was your war record, Prytherch?
I know: up and down the same field,
Following a horse; no oil for tractors;
Sniped at by rain, but never starving.
Did you listen to the reports
Of how heroes are fashioned and how killed?
Did you wait up late for the news?
Your world was the same world as before
Wars were contested, noisier only
Because of the echoes in the sky.
The blast worried your hair on its way to the hill;
The distances were a wound
Opened each night. Yet in your acres,
With no medals to be won,
You were on the old side of life,
Helping it in through the dark door
Of earth and beast, quietly repairing
The rents of history with your hands.

R. S. Thomas

THE FACE

When I close my eyes, I can see it,
That bare hill with the man ploughing,
Corrugating that brown roof
Under a hard sky. Under him is the farm,
Anchored in its grass harbour;
And below that the valley
Sheltering its few folk,
With the school and the inn and the church,
The beginning, middle and end
Of their slow journey above ground.

He is never absent, but like a slave
Answers to the mind's bidding,
Endlessly ploughing, as though autumn
Were the one season he knew.
Sometimes he pauses to look down
To the grey farmhouse, but no signals
Cheer him; there is no applause
For his long wrestling with the angel
Of no name. I can see his eye
That expects nothing, that has the rain's
Colourlessness. His hands are broken
But not his spirit. He is like bark
Weathering on the tree of his kind.

He will go on; that much is certain.
Beneath him tenancies of the fields
Will change; machinery turn
All to noise. But on the walls
Of the mind's gallery that face
With the hills framing it will hang
Unglorified, but stern like the soil.

R. S. Thomas

DIALECTIC

I would make a clear statement,
I would say that God is
More than the total of our spent prayers;
That minds indentured only by silence
Are a sure proof of what He is not.

Which is what Davies was saying
In his never to be published thesis,
Committed to memory by a single order
Of thrushes, vocal in the yew.

R. S. Thomas

IN CHURCH

Often I try
To analyse the quality
Of its silences. It this where God hides
From my searching? I have stopped to listen,
After the few people have gone,
To the air recomposing itself
For vigil. It has waited like this
Since the stones grouped themselves about it.
These are the hard ribs
Of a body that our prayers have failed
To animate. Shadows advance
From their corners to take possession
Of places the light held
For an hour. The bats resume
Their business. The uneasiness of the pews
Ceases. There is no other sound
In the darkness but the sound of a man
Breathing, testing his faith
On emptiness, nailing his questions
One by one to an untenanted cross.

R. S. Thomas

THE BELFRY

I have seen it standing up grey,
Gaunt, as though no sunlight
Could ever thaw out the music
Of its great bell; terrible
In its own way, for religion
Is like that. There are times
When a black frost is upon

One's whole being, and the heart
In its bone belfry hangs and is dumb.

But who is to know? Always,
Even in winter in the cold
Of a stone church, on his knees
Someone is praying, whose prayers fall
Steadily through the hard spell
Of weather that is between God
And himself. Perhaps they are warm rain
That brings the sun and afterwards flowers
On the raw graves and throbbing of bells.

R. S. Thomas

THE MOOR

It was like a church to me.
I entered it on soft foot,
Breath held like a cap in the hand.
It was quiet.
What God was there made himself felt,
Not listened to, in clean colours
That brought a moistening of the eye,
In movement of the wind over grass.

There were no prayers said. But stillness
Of the heart's passions—that was praise
Enough; and the mind's cession
Of its kingdom. I walked on,
Simple and poor, while the air crumbled
And broke on me generously as bread.

R. S. Thomas

AT ASQEFAR

At Asqefar the German helmet
Rests like a scarecrow's bonnet
On a bare branch.
The shreds of coarse grey duffel
Hang round the gap a rifle
Left in a shallow trench.

'Much blood,' said the shepherd,
Gesturing with his head
Towards the bald hillside.
A spent cartridge nestles
Among the dry thistles.
Blood long since dried.

Strange and remote, almost,
As these old figures traced
In Asqefar's cave:
There, pictured in red clay,
Odysseus comes back from Troy
Near the German's grave.

Twenty-five years since the battle
Plucked up the sand and let it settle
On the German soldier.
Far away now the living, the dead,
Disarmed, unhelmeted,
At Troy, at Asqefar.

Anthony Thwaite

AT DUNWICH

Fifteen churches lie here
Under the North Sea;

Forty-five years ago
The last went down the cliff.
You can see, at low tide,
A mound of masonry
Chewed like a damp bun.

In the village now (if you call
Dunwich a village now,
With a handful of houses, one street,
And a shack for Tizer and tea)
You can ask an old man
To show you the stuff they've found
On the beach when there's been a storm:

Knife-blades, buckles and rings,
Enough coins to fill an old sock,
Badges that men wore
When they'd been on pilgrimage,
Armfuls of broken pots.
People cut bread, paid cash,
Buttoned up against the cold.

Fifteen churches, and men
In thousands working at looms,
And wives brewing up stews
In great grey cooking pots.
I put out a hand and pull
A sherd from the cliff's jaws.
The sand trickles, then falls.

Nettles grow on the cliffs
In clumps as high as a house.
The houses have gone away.
Stand and look at the sea
Eating the land as it walks
Steadily treading the tops
Of fifteen churches' spires.

Anthony Thwaite

THE BARROW

In this high field strewn with stones
I walk by a green mound,
Its edges sheared by the plough.
Crumbs of animal bone
Lie smashed and scattered round
Under the clover leaves
And slivers of flint seem to grow
Like white leaves among green.
In the wind, the chestnut heaves
Where a man's grave has been.

Whatever the barrow held
Once, has been taken away:
A hollow of nettles and dock
Lies at the centre, filled
With rain from a sky so grey
It reflects nothing at all.
I poke in the crumbled rock
For something they left behind
But after that funeral
There is nothing at all to find.

On the map in front of me
The gothic letters pick out
Dozens of tombs like this,
Breached, plundered, left empty,
No fragments littered about
Of a dead and buried race
In the margins of histories.
No fragments: these splintered bones
Construct no human face,
These stones are simply stones.

In museums their urns lie
Behind glass, and their shaped flints

Are labelled like butterflies.
All that they did was die,
And all that has happened since
Means nothing to this place.
Above long clouds, the skies
Turn to a brilliant red
And show in the water's face
One living, and not these dead.

Anthony Thwaite

HEDGEHOG

Twitching the leaves just where the drainpipe clogs
In ivy leaves and mud, a purposeful
Creature at night about its business. Dogs
Fear his stiff seriousness. He chews away

At beetles, worms, slugs, frogs. Can kill a hen
With one snap of his jaws, can taunt a snake
To death on muscled spines. Old countrymen
Tell tales of hedgehogs sucking a cow dry.

But this one, cramped by houses, fences, walls,
Must have slept here all winter in that heap
Of compost, or have inched by intervals
Through tidy gardens to this ivy bed.

And here, dim-eyed, but ears so sensitive
A voice within the house can make him freeze,
He scuffs the edge of danger; yet can live
Happily in our nights and absences.

A country creature, wary, quiet and shrewd,
He takes the milk we give him, when we're gone.
At night, our slamming voices must seem crude
To one who sits and waits for silences.

Anthony Thwaite

252

COUNTY HOTEL, EDINBURGH

'Miss Minnes spends each winter with us here:
October through to May.' In the lounge
Miss Minnes sits and knots her hair
Through two bony fingers, and seems to cringe

When anyone walks by her. 'Yes, she comes
Of a very good family, up Inverness way.'
Miss Minnes sits doing complicated sums,
Dressed in a leather jerkin, day after day.

'She never speaks to anyone.' Long white face
Where eyes lie sunk in dreams, or maybe not.
In the television parlour she takes her place
For a minute or two, and then stalks out to sit

In the lounge and knot her hair and stare, stare
At the two electric bars which warm the room
From October through to May. If people cared
For Miss Minnes's seventy years, would she assume

They only meddled? 'Money's no object there.'
Among the debris of *The Field*, *The Sphere*
And last week's *Scotsman*, she, with lank grey hair,
Sits silent, twitching, winter by wintry year.

Anthony Thwaite

MAINE WINTER

Ravenous the flock
who with an artist's
tact, dispose
their crow-blue-black
over the spread of snow—

Trackless, save where
by stalled degrees
a fox flaringly goes
with more of the hunter's caution than
of the hunter's ease.

The flock
have sighted him, are his match
and more, with their artist's eye
and a score of beaks against
a fox, paws clogged, and a single pair of jaws.

And they mass to the red-on-white
conclusion, sweep
down between
a foreground all snow-scene and a distance
all cliff-tearing seascape.

Charles Tomlinson

LAS TRAMPAS U.S.A.

For Robert and Priscilla Bunker

I go through hollyhocks
in a dry garden, up
to the house,
knock, then ask
in English for the key
to Las Trampas church.
The old woman
says in Spanish: I
do not speak English
so I say: Where
is the church key

in Spanish.
—You see those
three men working: you
ask them. She
goes in, I
go on
preparing to ask
them in Spanish:
Hi, they say
in American. Hello
I say and ask
them in English
where is the key
to the church and they
say: He has it
gesturing to a fourth
man working
hoeing a corn-field
nearby, and to him
(in Spanish): Where is
the church key? And he:
I have it.—O.K.
they say in
Spanish-American:
You bring it (and
to me in English)
He'll bring it. You
wait for him
by the church door.
Thank you, I say and they
reply in American
You're welcome. I go
once more and
await in shadow
the key: he
who brings it is not
he of the hoe, but

one of the three
men working, who
with a Castilian grace
ushers me in
to this place
of coolness out
of the August sun.

Charles Tomlinson

ARIZONA DESERT

Eye
drinks the dry orange ground,
the cowskull
bound to it by shade:
sun-warped, the layers
of flaked and broken bone
unclench into petals,
into eyelids of limestone:

Blind glitter
that sees
spaces and steppes expand
of the purgatories possible
to us and
impossible.

Upended trees
in the Hopi's desert orchard
betoken
unceasing unspoken war,
return
the levelling light,
imageless arbiter.

A dead snake
pulsates again
as, hidden, the beetles' hunger
mines through the tunnel of its drying skin.

Here, to be,
is to sound
patience deviously
and follow
like the irregular corn
the water underground.

Villages
from mud and stone
parch back
to the dust they humanize
and mean

marriage, a loving lease
on sand, sun, rock and
Hopi
means peace.

Charles Tomlinson

THE DEATH OF BIRDS

I dreamt last night that our sick rain
Struck at the birds. It was a random thing,
Without a tremble some would drop in flight.
The twisted, stiffening bodies lay about
My mother's lawn. One dead thrush gaped its jaw.
My living children cried at what they saw.

So past and future and the dying birds
Were all my dream; and with these images
Haunted my waking thoughts throughout the day.
Then I remembered those old stories which
Told of the heroes saved from danger, when
Birds gave a warning understood by men.

And I remembered how the miners took
Small singing birds in cages underground,
Who died to show them when the poisoned air,
If they went on, would choke their breath up too.
And yet my dream was not explained by that.
Tonight I found a sparrow crushed quite flat.

Shirley Toulson

POMPEIAN DOG

Like that Pompeian dog chained to a stone
I howl as living cinders pour, half-blind
Howl as I search the cracking street to find
An answer to this freak of storms sky-thrown.
I howl, but cannot turn to blame
The hand that tied me to these gouts of death,
A sheet of cinders chars my staggered breath
Chained to a world of unforgiving flame.

C. A. Trypanis

DECEMBER TWENTY FOUR

Tonight it will turn to snow,
A glass lid covers the well,
The snail shrinks deep in his shell
And hungry starlings fly low.

And the shed's floor sourly iced
Clings to the hooves of the cattle,
The legs of dim-eyed sheep rattle—
A hard birth for Christ.

C. A. Trypanis

EASTER POEM

I had gone on Easter Day
early and alone to be
beyond insidious bells
(that any other Sunday
I'd not hear) up to the hills
where are winds to blow away

commination. In the frail
first light I saw him, unreal
and sudden through lifting mist,
a fox on a barn door, nailed
like a coloured plaster Christ
in a Spanish shrine, his tail

coiled around his loins. Sideways
his head hung limply, his ears
snagged with burdock, his dry nose
plugged with black blood. For two days
he'd held the orthodox pose.
The endemic English noise

of Easter Sunday morning
was mixed in the mist swirling
and might have moved his stiff head.
Under the hill the ringing
had begun: and the sun rose red
on the stains of his bleeding.

I walked the length of the day's
obsession. At dusk I was
swallowed by the misted barn,
sucked by the peristalsis
of my fear that he had gone,
leaving nails for souvenirs.

But he was there still. I saw
no sign. He hung as before.
Only the wind had risen
to comb the thorns from his fur.
I left my superstition
stretched on the banging barn door.

Ted Walker

STARLINGS

Our fears, like starlings, gather
with the dusk. Small particles
they come, innumerable,
flying direct from further
skies of mind only guessed at.
Wheeling, they circle us, squat

near. If ever a pair of birds
should strut a sunlit pavement
before us, caught in movement
of the day's concern, we goad
them, approach, put them to flight;
sometimes, even, feed them. But

lodged, untouchable by night,
in the high clerestories
of the stone-still, moon-carved trees

we move among, they will not
be put up at our passing
boldly under their roostings.

Sometimes we can keep away
through the long-lain night. Awake
we may avoid them, though flocks
heave throbbing through our dreams, high
in the misproportioned limbs
of our imaginings.

If we should decide to come
to them, hear their mummeries
mock us when one of them stirs
to ripple through all of them,
sacristan black, we may judge
their strength, though they will not budge

before the day. When they go
they leave uneasy calm, as
they turn as one like louvres,
letting the sunlight through.
And only the sense remains
of the black beneath the sheen

and the knowledge that the swift
and silent flight of other
birds, unseen, has passed over
us, sinister, borne aloft
by wings more menacing
yet than those of the known starling.

Ted Walker

CUCKOO-PINT

So cold now. I remember
you—bright hedgerow tarts you were,
flagrant in your big red beads,
cheerful, vulgar and brazen.
But then,

in a sudden October,
when the white night of winter
came, you put aside your gauds
and took vows. Now you open
again,

hooded, cool and sinister.
I know you for what you are
unveiled: loose, secular brides
frustrated with this convent
torment.

Ted Walker

CARP

By day falls the white blossom
of may on his olive back
inert on top like a rock.
Small silver shiners spin from
him as bright jangles of fry
veer from his stillness. But by

night, when bats bring their darkness
and start to sip at the pool
in a sideslip as they whirl
round the same two trees endlessly, come the night skirmishes.
He has been waiting for this.

It is as though night prises
a scale or two up. He bolts
through reeds to smoothen them; halts;
sucks the yellow irises
encrusted with yellow eggs.
He sucks till his belly sags,

as he quaffs in unison
with the cows' rough tongues ripping
grass at the edge. His sipping
admits a long procession
of passing flies. Then it stops.
He turns within his length, flaps

a gossamer from his fin,
and, exploiting his great strength,
hurls his amplitude the length
of a pond too small for him,
back and back and back again,
savaging the restriction

of lily stalks and the roots
where the lurking yellow perch
hover in amazement, arch-
ing their spines. And he starts
circuiting, circuiting, like
a brash skater at a rink,

trailing his barbels beneath
his gape as he goes, rejoic-
ing that he was made for this
alone, until the first breath
of a day breeze blows and quietly he attends a new night.

Ted Walker

A CHRISTMAS HYMN

And some of the Pharisees from among the multitude said unto him, Master, rebuke thy disciples.

And he answered and said unto them, I tell you that, if these should hold their peace, the stones would immediately cry out.

ST LUKE XIX, 39–40

A stable-lamp is lighted
Whose glow shall wake the sky;
The stars shall bend their voices,
And every stone shall cry.
And every stone shall cry,
And straw like gold shall shine;
A barn shall harbour heaven,
A stall become a shrine.

This child through David's city
Shall ride in triumph by;
The palm shall strew its branches,
And every stone shall cry.
And every stone shall cry,
Though heavy, dull, and dumb,
And lie within the roadway
To pave his kingdom come.

Yet he shall be forsaken,
And yielded up to die;
The sky shall groan and darken,
And every stone shall cry.
And every stone shall cry
For stony hearts of men:
God's blood upon the spearhead,
God's love refused again.

But now, as at the ending,
The low is lifted high;
The stars shall bend their voices,

And every stone shall cry.
And every stone shall cry
In praises of the child
By whose descent among us
The worlds are reconciled.

Richard Wilbur

ABORIGINE

He is only beautiful
In the manner of his country,
For he was burnt by the same enemy,
Was at the same treaty.

And now he lives on a concession
Which shifts with each season,
That he must follow it
As a jackal follows his lion,

Licking at gnawed bones
Till he himself is one,
Hollow and dry as an old tree,
Full of strange, delicate energy.

For he can walk a whole month
Into the desert in the dreamtime,
Can scent water on wind
And make rabbits jump into his hand.

He can hit a snake with a stone,
Birds with a boomerang;
Can play a long, sad note
And paint stories on bark,
Beautiful in the manner of his country.

Hugo Williams

THE HITCH HIKER

I have waited days
Beside roads in Queensland,
Got to know their ways.

I am familiar with
Their bric-à-brac, pierced
Beer cans, combs, old hats,

Salvage of picnics, breakdowns,
Love affairs, scraps
Of women's weeklies, used perhaps
For sandwiches, or worse.

The Townsville Times, September 10,
Carried an item on Floyd Paterson.

What year would that be?
Things seem to last indefinitely
Under the bone-dry dust
Of a thousand travelling salesmen.

Roadsides are desert islands. There
You are cast up like driftwood,
Dependent on the tides and moods
Of motorists, and there you stay,

Flotsam and jetsam of the highway.

Hugo Williams

ROUEN

Why did no-one say it
was like this?
These cobbles smoking

still with the shame of her burning,
and the mediaeval houses leaning
    with shuttered eyes
    and shuddered looks.

Today the people are unreal
they are the shadows
who drift the square.
Only the ghosts live. Their spirits
clamour for our attention, the guilty
    soldiers shout
    the silent crowds cry out.

There is a market behind
her white statue,
the suppliant stone
compels the clamorous thoughts
of butter and Normandy cheese bought
    with frugal care,
    to an awareness of prayer.

At her feet are flowers,
flat little wreaths
where the flames licked
first, of the country flowers she knew
and must have loved when child she grew
    so soon to a saint's
    stature and restraint.

She must have been
a difficult person
to live with, knowing
herself to be right, having her voices
at her elbow. The people had no choice
    but to call her
    witch, and staked, burn her.

Even now, it is awkward
being English, and taking
photographs. We speak
French, quietly, hoping we are unnoticed. They
did not put in the Guide that the grey
     square still cried
     so long after she died.

Marguerite Wood

WHAT MATTERED

The King rode down to the bridge
for his triumphal entry,
his horse leaving deep impressions in the road
like the marks of a giant's fingers.
The crowds cheered him across
—he made it, though it cracked under him,
for he was able to lift himself a little forward.
The maidens' faces,
pretty as rows of little pink shells,
gave him smiles;
his soldiers, helmeted like whelks,
stood at attention round the gate.
Half-way through the arch
he doubled back and jumped over the wall
to land inside.
The wild huzzas went on,
for no one noticed.
They knew what mattered.

The bowls of the fountains, mother-of-pearl,
on each side of the way (paved with pebbles)
slid back iridescent gleams as he moved on.
At the beginning of the spiral ramp

of the central keep
two marble columns stood,
finely etched by his craftsmen with mounting arcs
so that they looked like razor-shells on end.

No one noticed either
when going up the ramp
every time he got round to the left-hand side
he was twisted
and had to jump back to put himself right.

He reached the top,
acknowledging the loyal roar
from the empty square.

No one noticed his legs were fingers,
his body a hand.
The child whose hand it was
knew what mattered.

*   *   *   *   *

Next day
where the sandcastle had been
was a shining slope
being smoothed again and again
by the waves.
No one noticed.
They knew what mattered.

Edmond Leo Wright

NOVEMBER GHOST

The garden has a yellow stamp
This time of the year and the day;
With my reflected lamp

In the window, like a holiday
Lantern in mid-air, I am neither
Indoors nor out, but on whisper
Terms with this delicate damp
Weather, this secret November.

The trees are bare, the poplar
And the elder, but the evergreen
Bushes this evening look the colder,
Dark and huddled in cloaks. The tambourine
Ping of a one-toned vesper bell
Tongues the congealing air: again the festival
Breaks in, uncertain of the time of the year
Or the day, and in the shrubs some animal

That would not in the farmyard linger, pell-mell
Streaking through, stops here wheezing like a jester.
It softens winter and is whimsical
To think this time digresses for fiesta.
Therefore in summer the real moon will but seem
Hung up, and that field creature in rheum
Will hiccup under the dance-tune. This fall
Will trouble me like a recurring dream.

Lotte Zurndorfer

ACKNOWLEDGMENTS

Thanks are due to the authors (or their executors), their representatives and publishers mentioned in the following list for their kind permission to reproduce copyright material:

A. R. Ammons: 'Mission' (published in *Poetry*, Vol. 110, No. 3, June 1967).

Carroll Arnett: 'Bushmills', 'The Dare' and 'Next' from *Not Only That* (Elizabeth Press).

Michael Baldwin: 'Economic Cosmohagiography' from *How Charles Egget Lost His Way in a Creation Myth* (Secker and Warburg Ltd); 'Wasdale Head Church, 1957' from *Death on a Live Wire and On Stepping from a Sixth-Storey Window* (Longman Group Ltd).

Patricia Beer: 'The Postilion Has Been Struck by Lightning', 'Four Years After', 'Armistice Day' and 'Abbey Tomb' from *Just Like the Resurrection* (Macmillan and Co. Ltd and Macmillan Company of Canada Ltd).

Martin Bell: 'Reasons for Refusal', 'Senilio's Weather Saw' and 'Ultimate Anthology' from *Collected Poems, 1937–1966* (Macmillan and Co. Ltd, St Martin's Press Inc. and Macmillan Company of Canada Ltd).

Anne Beresford: 'The Romanies in Town' from *The Lair* (Rapp and Whiting Ltd).

Francis Berry: 'Gudveig' from *The Ghosts of Greenland* (Routledge and Kegan Paul Ltd).

John Betjeman: 'Inexpensive Progress', 'Harvest Hymn', 'Lines written to Martyn Skinner before his departure from Oxfordshire in search of quiet—1961', 'By the Ninth Green, St Enodoc', 'Cornish Cliffs' and 'Agricultural Caress' from *High and Low* (John Murray (Publishers) Ltd).

D. M. Black: 'The Educators' from *The Educators* (The Cresset Press Ltd).

Thomas Blackburn: 'Home, Home on the Range' from *Snakes and Ladders* (MacGibbon and Kee Ltd).

John Blight: 'Death of a Whale' from *A Beachcomber's Diary* (Angus and Robertson Ltd).

Frederick Bock: 'October Silence' (published in *Poetry*, Vol. 102, No. 4, July 1963).

Alan Bold: 'On Seeing Voskhod Over Edinburgh' from *To Find the New* (Chatto and Windus Ltd).

Edwin Brock: '5 Ways to Kill a Man' and 'On Being Chosen for a Schools Anthology' from *With Love from Judas* (Scorpion Press); 'Symbols of the Sixties' and 'A Moment of Respect' from *Penguin Modern Poets 8* (Penguin Books Ltd).

Arthur J. Bull: 'Richness', 'Leaves', 'Nature' and 'The Wind' from *Selected Poems* (Outposts Publications).

Kenneth Burke: 'And Here I Am, Fighting Dandelions' and 'Heavy Heavy—What Hangs Over?' from *Collected Poems* (University of California Press Inc). By permission of the Regents of the University of California.

Miles Burrows: 'Economics', 'Odysseus' and 'Troy' from *A Vulture's Egg* (Jonathan Cape Ltd).

Philip Callow: 'A Frosty Night' from *Turning Point* (William Heinemann Ltd); 'Monday Snowfall' from *The Real Life* (Times Press Ltd, Douglas, Isle of Man).

Charles Causley: 'By St Thomas Water', 'Reservoir Street', 'School at Four O'Clock', 'Death of a Poet', 'Lord Sycamore', 'Ballad of the Bread Man' and 'Immunity' from *Underneath the Water* (Macmillan and Co. Ltd and Macmillan Company of Canada Ltd); 'Guy Fawkes' Day' and 'Grave by the Sea' from *Johnny Alleluia* (Rupert Hart-Davis Ltd).

Richard Church: 'The Last Freedom', 'The Recognition' and 'The Camel' from *The Burning Bush, Poems 1958–1966* (William Heinemann Ltd).

Austin Clarke: 'A Strong Wind' and 'Medical Missionary of Mary' from *Flight to Africa* (Dolmen Press Ltd).

Stewart Conn: 'Under Creag Mhor', 'Bowling Green, Troon' and 'Summer Farm' from *Thunder in the Air* (Akros Publications); 'Flight' and ' The Orchard' from *Stoats in the Sunlight* (Hutchinson and Co. (Publishers) Ltd).

Tony Connor: 'Above Penmaenmawr' and 'Druid's Circle' from *Kon in Springtime* and 'Elegy for Alfred Hubbard' from *With Love Somehow* (Oxford University Press).

E. E. Cummings: Poems 42, 43, 44 and 53 from *Complete Poems 1913–1963* (MacGibbon and Kee Ltd).

C. Day-Lewis: 'The Fox' from *The Room* (Jonathan Cape Ltd).

Paul Dehn: 'O Nuclear Wind', 'Ring-a-ring', 'Rain Before Seven', 'I Had a Little Shadow', 'Rock of Ages', 'As with Gladness' and 'Onward, Christian Soldiers' from *Quake, Quake, Quake* and 'Gutter Press' from *The Fern on the Rock* (Hamish Hamilton Ltd). Copyright © Paul Dehn 1965 (Illustrations by Edward Gorey).

Patric Dickinson: 'The World I See' from *The World I See* and 'A New Block' and 'This Cold Universe' from *This Cold Universe* (Chatto and Windus Ltd).

Rosemary Dobson: 'Jack' from *Cockcrow* (Angus and Robertson Ltd).

Clifford Dyment: 'Prayer', 'Sea Shanty', 'Outlaw' and 'The Desert'.

Brian Earnshaw: 'Mock Examinations', 'Meeting People on Dowrog', 'Staff Lunch' and 'Senior Debating' from *At St David's a Year* (Hodder and Stoughton Ltd).

Marguerite Edmonds: 'The Old Ladies' (published in *Outposts*) and 'Pallor of Angels' (published in *Poésie Vivante* and *New Measure*).

Julian Ennis: 'Cold Storage'.

D. J. Enright: 'Apocalypse', 'Village Classes' and 'Pitchfork Department' from *Addictions* (Chatto and Windus Ltd).

Gavin Ewart: 'The Middle Years' from *Pleasures of the Flesh* (Alan Ross Ltd).

Janet Frame: 'The Dead', 'Complaint', 'Autumn' and 'Sunday' from *The Pocket Mirror* (W. H. Allen and Co. Ltd).

Robin Fulton: 'The End of an Age', 'A Note for Robert Henryson' and 'The Snake' from *Instances* (M. Macdonald, Edinburgh, 1967).

Karen Gershon: 'Race' and 'In a Tram' from *Selected Poems* (Victor Gollancz Ltd).

Zulfikar Ghose: 'The Crows' from *The Loss of India* (Routledge and Kegan Paul Ltd).

David Gill: 'The Mission' from *Men Without Evenings* (Chatto and Windus Ltd).

Robert Graves: 'The Two Witches' and 'The Hung Wu Vase' from *Collected Poems 1965* (Cassell and Co. Ltd).

Bryn Griffiths: 'Ianto the Undertaker' from *The Stones Remember* (J. M. Dent and Sons Ltd); 'A Note for R. S. Thomas'.

Charles Gullans: 'Autumn Day · Rainer Maria Rilke' and 'The Sovereign Hotel, Santa Monica' from *Arrivals and Departures* (University of Minnesota Press Inc).

Donald Hall: 'By the North Sea' and 'The Poem' from *A Roof of Tiger Lilies* (Andre Deutsch Ltd).

Michael Hamburger: 'Omens' and 'Security' from *Weather and Season* (Longman Group Ltd).

George Rostrevor Hamilton: 'Terra Incognita' from *Landscape of the Mind* (William Heinemann Ltd).

Seamus Heaney: 'Turkeys Observed', 'Docker' and 'The Play Way' from *Death of a Naturalist* (Faber and Faber Ltd).

John Heath-Stubbs: 'The Bed Bug', 'The Starling', 'The Tortoise' and 'Poetry Today' from *The Blue-Fly in His Head* (Oxford University Press).

Antony Hecht: 'It Out-Herods Herod. Pray You, Avoid It.' from *The Hard Hours* (Oxford University Press).

Phoebe Hesketh: 'Admarsh Church Bleasdale', 'The Fox', 'The Frog Prince' and 'The Dark Side of the Moon' from *Prayer for the Sun* (Rupert Hart-Davis Ltd).

Philip Hobsbaum: 'Provincial Undergraduate' from *The Place's Fault and Other Poems* (Macmillan and Co. Ltd and Macmillan Company of Canada Ltd).

David Holliday: 'Logria' and 'Pompeii' (published in *Outposts*).

Mary Horton: 'The Song of the Spectators' and 'The Eavesdroppers' (published in *Outposts*).

Graham Hough: 'Awakening' and 'Death in the Village' from *Legends and Pastorals* (Gerald Duckworth and Co. Ltd).

Ted Hughes: 'Thistles' from *Wodwo* and 'Pike', 'Bullfrog', 'The Retired Colonel', 'Hawk Roosting' and 'Pennines in April' from *Lupercal* (Faber and Faber Ltd).

Ada Jackson: 'Church School' (published in P.E.N. *New Poems 1960*) and 'Our Brother Richard' (published in *Country Life* and P.E.N. *New Poems 1965*).

Randall Jarrell: 'The Bird of Night' from *The Lost World* (Eyre and Spottiswoode (Publishers) Ltd).

Elizabeth Jennings: 'The Young Ones' and 'Warning to Parents' from *Recoveries* (Andre Deutsch Ltd).

Brian Jones: 'Thaw' from *Poems* (London Magazine Editions).

Donald Justice: 'Counting the Mad' from *The Summer Anniversaries* (Wesleyan University Press Inc).

James Kirkup: 'Japanese Fan', 'Four Haiku on the Inland Sea', 'Sumo Wrestlers', 'Earthquake Dream', 'The Aerial Contortionist', 'Not Cricket' and 'Cena' from *Paper Windows* (J. M. Dent and Sons Ltd).

Felicia Lamport: 'Plaintive Geometry', 'Historical Survey' and '→Drawn Onward←' from *Cultural Slag* (Victor Gollancz Ltd). (Illustrations by Edward Gorey.)

Philip Larkin: 'An Arundel Tomb', 'MCMXIV' and 'Toads Revisited' from *The Whitsun Weddings* (Faber and Faber Ltd).

Laurie Lee: 'Fish and Water' from *London Magazine Poems 1961–1966* (London Magazine Editions).

Laurence Lerner: 'A Birthday Card to My Best Friend' and 'To School' from *The Directions of Memory, Poems 1958–1963* (Chatto and Windus Ltd).

Douglas Livingstone: 'Vulture' and 'Sunstrike' from *Sjambok* (Oxford University Press).

Christopher Logue: 'Professor Tuholsky's Facts'.

Edward Lucie-Smith: 'The Barbarian Invasions' from *Confessions and Histories* and 'The Witnesses' and 'Salisbury Plain' from *A Tropical Childhood and Other Poems* (Oxford University Press).

George MacBeth: 'Bedtime Story' from *The Broken Places* and 'The Red Herring' from *A Doomsday Book* (Scorpion Press); 'Bats' from *The Colour of Blood* (Macmillan and Co. Ltd and Macmillan Company of Canada Ltd).

Norman MacCaig: 'Frogs' from *Surroundings* and 'Solitary Crow', 'Starlings' and 'Crossing the Border' from *Rings on a Tree* (Chatto and Windus Ltd).

Donagh MacDonagh: 'Just an Old Sweet Song' from *A Warning to Conquerors* (Dolmen Press Ltd).

Derek Mahon: 'My Wicked Uncle' from *Night Crossing* (Oxford University Press).

Dom Moraes: 'Christmas Sonnets: I Santa Claus; II Family Dinner' from *John Nobody* (Eyre and Spottiswoode (Publishers) Ltd).

Robert Morgan: 'The Cwm Above Penrhiwceiber', 'Low Seam

Miner' and 'Huw's Farm' from *The Night's Prison* (Rupert Hart-Davis Ltd).

Richard Murphy: 'Droit de Seigneur · 1820' from *Sailing to an Island* (Faber and Faber Ltd).

Howard Nemerov: 'A Spell Before Winter', 'The Companions' and 'Grace to be Said at the Supermarket' from *The Winter Lightning* (Rapp and Whiting Ltd).

Francis Newbold: 'Speech Day' (published in *Outposts*).

Norman Nicholson: 'The Elvers', 'The Cock's Nest', 'On the Closing of Millom Ironworks: September 1968', 'Have You Been to London?' and 'A Local Preacher's Goodbye' (The Poetry Book Society, the Editors of *Stand*, *English*, and *The Transatlantic Review*).

John Normanton: 'Splendid Girls' from *London Magazine Poems 1961–1966* (London Magazine Editions).

Robert Pack: 'The Monster Who Loved the Hero' from *Selected Poems* (Chatto and Windus Ltd).

Paul Petrie: 'The Miners' (published in *Outposts*).

Sylvia Plath: 'Cut' from *Ariel* and 'Snakecharmer' from *The Colossus* (Faber and Faber Ltd). By permission of Ted Hughes.

William Plomer: 'Mrs Middleditch' from *Taste and Remember* (Jonathan Cape Ltd); 'Before the Crash' from *London Magazine Poems 1961–1966* (London Magazine Editions).

Peter Porter: 'Your Attention Please' from *Once Bitten, Twice Bitten* (Scorpion Press).

Frank Prewett: 'Blackbird' from *Collected Poems* (Cassell and Co. Ltd). By permission of the Executor of the Estate of Frank Prewett.

John Pudney: 'Twentieth-century Mother' from *Spill Out* (J. M. Dent and Sons Ltd).

Peter Redgrove: 'Spider' from *The Nature of Cold Weather and Other Poems* (Routledge and Kegan Paul Ltd).

James Reeves: 'Spicer's Instant Poetry' from *The Questioning Tiger* (William Heinemann Ltd); 'The Travellers'.

Theodore Roethke: 'The Pike', 'Heard in a Violent Ward', 'The Geranium' and 'Elegy' from *Collected Poems* (Faber and Faber Ltd).

Alan Ross: 'Autostrada del Sole' and 'Near Carthage' from *Poems 1942–1967* (Eyre and Spottiswoode (Publishers) Ltd).

Vernon Scannell: 'Walking Wounded', 'Autumn' and 'Ruminant' from *Walking Wounded* (Eyre and Spottiswoode (Publishers) Ltd); 'Ageing Schoolmaster', 'Autobiographical Note', 'Remembrance Day', 'The Great War' and 'The Men Who Wear My Clothes'.

Howard Sergeant: 'Strategy' (published in *Poetry India*).

Anne Sexton: 'A Curse against Elegies', 'Lullaby' and 'Ringing the Bells' from *Selected Poems* (Oxford University Press).

Alan Sillitoe: 'Woods' from *A Falling Out of Love and Other Poems* and 'Poem Written in Majorca' and 'Carthage' from *The Rats* (W. H. Allen and Co. Ltd).

Louis Simpson: 'American Poetry', 'Frogs' and 'The Redwoods' from *Selected Poems* (Oxford University Press).

Edith Sitwell: 'The War Orphans' from *The Outcasts* (Macmillan and Co. Ltd).

Robin Skelton: 'West Penwith' from *Begging the Dialect* (Oxford University Press).

Iain Crichton Smith: 'Rythm' from *The Law and the Grace* (Eyre and Spottiswoode (Publishers) Ltd); 'At the Highland Games' (published in *Lines Review*).

Ken Smith: 'Both Harvests' from *The Pity* (Jonathan Cape Ltd).

Stevie Smith: 'Bog-Face', 'At School' and 'The Grange' from *The Frog Prince and Other Poems* (Longman Group Ltd).

Bernard Spencer: 'A Sunday' from *Collected Poems* (Alan Ross Ltd).

Jon Stallworthy: 'Shall These Bones Live?' and 'Romance' from *The Astronomy of Love* and 'First Blood', 'Then', ' "Here Comes Sir George" ', 'No Ordinary Sunday' and 'Camel' from *Out of Bounds* (Oxford University Press).

Gordon Symes: 'Town and Country' (published in *Outposts*).

A. S. J. Tessimond: 'In Canterbury Cathedral' (published in *The Listener*). By permission of the Literary Executor, Hubert Nicholson; 'Heaven' from *London Magazine Poems 1961–1966* (London Magazine Editions).

D. M. Thomas: 'Limbo' from *Penguin Modern Poets 11* (Penguin Books Ltd).

Donald Thomas: 'Lizard' and 'Tangier: Hotel Rif' from *Points of Contact* (Routledge and Kegan Paul Ltd).

R. S. Thomas: 'Afforestation', 'A Country' and 'Truth' from *The Bread of Truth*; 'Hireling', 'Portrait' and 'Dialectic' from *Tares*; 'For the Record', 'The Face', 'In Church', 'The Belfry' and 'The Moor' from *Pieta* (Rupert Hart-Davis Ltd).

Anthony Thwaite: 'At Asqefar' and 'At Dunwich' from *The Stones of Happiness* and 'The Barrow', 'Hedgehog' and 'County Hotel, Edinburgh' from *The Owl in the Tree* (Oxford University Press).

Charles Tomlinson: 'Maine Winter', 'Las Trampas U.S.A.' and 'Arizona Desert' from *American Scenes* (Oxford University Press).

Shirley Toulson: 'The Death of Birds' from *Shadows in an Orchard* (Scorpion Press).

C. A. Trypanis: 'Pompeian Dog' and 'December Twenty Four' from *Pompeian Dog* (Faber and Faber Ltd).

Ted Walker: 'Easter Poem', 'Starlings', 'Cuckoo-pint' and 'Carp' from *Fox on a Barn Door* (Jonathan Cape Ltd).

Richard Wilbur: 'A Christmas Hymn' from *Advice to a Prophet* (Faber and Faber Ltd).

Hugo Williams: 'Aborigine' and 'The Hitch Hiker' from *Symptoms of Loss* (Oxford University Press).

Marguerite Wood: 'Rouen' from *The Stone of Vision* (Outposts Publications).

Edmond Leo Wright: 'What Mattered' (published in P.E.N. *New Poems 1967*).

Lotte Zurndorfer: 'November Ghost' from *Poems* (Chatto and Windus Ltd).

INDEX OF THEMES

This is a personal selection. Some poems are included under more than one heading; some are not included at all, since they do not belong to any of these categories.